Presentation Skills for Prosperity

A Network Marketer's Guide to Giving 1-to-1 and Group Presentations that Sky Rocket Your Success

Carla Rieger
©2016

If you would like access to our FREE Presenter Personality Style Quiz go here:
http://carlarieger.com/MLMDANCEQUIZ

Presentation Skills for Prosperity

Legal Disclaimer

Copyright © 2016 Carla Rieger. All rights reserved worldwide.

No part of this material may be used, reproduced, distributed or transmitted in any form and by any means whatsoever, including without limitation photocopying, recording or other electronic or mechanical methods or by any information storage and retrieval system, without the prior written permission from the author, except for brief excerpts in a review.

This book is intended to provide general information only. Neither the author nor publisher provide any legal or other professional advice. If you need professional advice, you should seek advice from the appropriate licensed professional. This book does not provide complete information on the subject matter covered. This book is not intended to address specific requirements, either for an individual or an organization. This book is intended to be used only as a general guide, and not as a sole source of information on the subject matter. While the author has undertaken diligent efforts to ensure accuracy, there is no guarantee of accuracy or of no errors, omissions or typographical errors. Any slights of people or organizations are unintentional. The author and publisher shall have no liability or responsibility to any person or entity and hereby disclaim all liability, including without limitation, liability for consequential damages regarding any claim, loss or damage that may be incurred, or alleged to have been incurred, directly or indirectly, arising out of the information provided in this book.

Connect with Carla
www.CarlaRieger.com
https://www.facebook.com/carlarieger
https://twitter.com/carlarieger
https://www.instagram.com/riegercarla
https://es.pinterest.com/carlarieger/
https://www.linkedin.com/in/carlarieger

Copyright © 2016 by Carla Rieger
All rights reserved. No part of this publication may be reproduced or transmitted in any form or by any means, electronic, or mechanical, including photocopying, recording, or by any information storage and retrieval system.

The Artistry of Change Training & Consulting Inc.
Visit us on the web: www.ArtistryofChange.com
E-Mail: Carla@ArtistryofChange.com

Dedication/Acknowledgement

During the many years that it took me to research and write this book so many people supported me on the journey. I had the privilege of crossing paths with literally hundreds of people who have made my life richer and who influenced the course of this book.

I would like to thank my awesome life and business partner, Dave O'Connor, for his loving presence in my life. I would never have gotten to where I am today without his amazing support and brilliant vision. Also I want to thank my sister, Lorraine McGregor, and my parents Ann and Harry Rieger for their continued support of my exploration into public speaking and theatre, even at an early age.

Playfair Inc. and in particular Matt Weinstein, Jerry Ewen and Carol Ann Fried for inviting me into the world of professional speaking while I was still in college.

In addition, these groups helped me grow and learn much faster than I could do by myself as a presenter and performer:
- The Canadian Association of Professional Speakers
- The Professional Speakers Association of UK
- The National Speakers Association of the US
- The Women Speakers Association
- Rapid Time Network

- Applied Improvisation Network
- Theatresports
- Second City
- The eWomen Network
- The Mastery Community

All my writing, acting and dramaturge mentors such as Paula Shaw, Jonathan Fox, Stanley Weiss, Gina Bastone, Arina Issacson, Linda Darlow, Larry Gilman, Alex Bruhanski, Michael Shurleff, Michael Berry, Patricia Dahlquist, Ian Raffel, and Marc Baur.

And of course my brilliant collaborator on this book, Kim Thompson-Pinder!

And finally, all my presentation skills clients who, over all these years, taught me so much about what it takes to shine as a presenter.

Presentation Skills for Prosperity

Table of Contents

Presentation Skills for Prosperity 1
Legal Disclaimer 2
Dedication/Acknowledgement 3
Table of Contents 5
Chapter 1: Who Should Read This Book 7
    Is this Book for You? 8
    My Background 10
Chapter 2: Introduction 15
    Different Types of Presentations 16
    Sharing Stories vs. Sharing Concepts 17
    What Makes a Story Relatable? 20

SECTION 1: GETTING READY FOR YOUR PRESENTATION 25
Chapter 3: The All Important 27
Ground Work 27
    Presentation Goals Clarity Process 29
    Answering Questions About Your Life 31
    Choosing the Right Niche & Finding Hungry Prospects within that Niche 34
    Structuring Your Presentation 36
    Timeline of a 60 Minute Presentation 39
Chapter 4: Story Basics 45
    The Hero's Journey 46
    The Ascension Structure: A 5 Part Process 48
Chapter 5: The Power of Creating Your Why Story 53
    My WHY Story 55
    Creating Your Why Story 60
    Rita's Story 68
    What's Next? 72
Chapter 6: Two Short Presentations Every Network Marketer Needs 75
    Your Mission Statement 76
    Pitching A Network Marketing Business Opportunity 78
    Business Opportunity Example 82

SECTION 2: PRESENTATION TIME 87
Chapter 7: How to Avoid the Top 4 Mistakes Presenters Make 89
    Mistake #1 - Not Caring About Your Audience 90
    Mistake #2- Resisting People's Resistance 97

Mistake # 3 - Lack of Proper Rehearsal 99
Mistake #4 - Trying to Do It Alone...103
Chapter 8 - How to Transform Anxiety as a Presenter 105
Mistake #1 – Comparing Yourself Negatively to Others 107
Mistake #2 – Allowing Negative Self Talk to Take Over 108
My Story of Transformation 114
Chapter 9: Captivating Your Audience...119
Left Brain/Right Brain Dominance 120
V.A.R.K. 124
Getting Better Results 126
Chapter 10: Putting It All Together..127
It's A Process 127
The Checklist 128
Who Is Carla Rieger? 132

Chapter 1: Who Should Read This Book

Sonya's heart was pounding with fear and excitement as she waited for an old friend who was supposed to meet her for coffee. For months she had been trying to build her network marketing business on her own with very poor results. Now she was getting training. She was actually learning what it takes to give powerful presentations, and today was the moment of truth. Would the training pay off?

When her friend arrived, they caught up for a few minutes and then she talked about her company. By the end of the conversation, her friend was genuinely interested in hearing more about joining! Sonya invited her to a meeting (which she showed up for) and started her business that evening.

After months of struggling to learn how to enroll someone into her company, (all that time thinking that she was a failure), she discovered it came down to shifting her mindset habits and learning a few simple presentation skills. That's what helped her get her first team member.

From then on there was nothing that could stop Sonya, she was always learning more about building healthy mindset habits and presenting her opportunity in the right way, and the results showed it. Every month, she was adding more people to her team. Over time she grew from coffee shops to home meetings, to hotel meetings, then webinars and videos. Three years later, she was one of the top leaders in her company and speaking on stage at their annual convention. All from learning a few of the things you're going to learn in this book.

Is this Book for You?

When most people think of the word 'presentation, they think 'public speaking.' However, that is just one form of presentation. There are many other forms that are effective for building your business and we will cover them in this book.

If you are not sure if this book applies to you, then answer these questions below:

> **1. Do you regularly talk to people face-to-face about your business?** For example, at networking

events, dinner parties or the playground with other parents. You know, when someone says, "So, what do you do?" Then, you've got 30 seconds to get them interested. It's one of the hardest presentations to do and how well you do it can make or break your business growth.

2. Do you speak on the phone to leads? That is another form of presentation. While it may seem more like a conversation, HOW you add your business presentation into that conversation, is very important. It really should be something that is a combo of both scripted and spontaneous. So, on the one hand, you're not just totally "winging" it, but on the other hand, you're not coming across as too scripted and wooden.

3. Do you post content online? For example, maybe you send emails, post photos, add social media comments, create videos, teleseminars or webinars to entice people to learn more about your company. This is another form of presentation that can yield huge results if done well.

4. Do you want to better motivate and mentor your team? Maybe you watch other leaders who can get their team to accomplish great things just by talking to them, and you want to be more like that. And finally…

5. **Do you speak to groups of people?** That can be as little as five people or as large as hundreds. Do you want to give presentations that catch people's attention and make them want to take action?

If you said yes to any of these questions, then this book is for you. It doesn't matter what level you are at; you will learn new skills to take your presentations to a whole other level of excellence. And these skills will serve you not only in your network marketing business, but in all areas of life.

My Background

Most people think that I must have been a natural born speaker, but that wasn't the case. I was terrified of public speaking. I was shy and introverted. I would have stayed that way, except for a invitation from a friend. While in university, I got invited by two friends to join a training company. They told me that my job would be to stand up in front of hundreds [and sometimes thousands] of college freshmen and present to them.

The goals would be to get new students excited about being on campus and open to meeting other students. For example, I would say "go find two other people in the room wearing the same color as you and find out their home town!" Or, "Form a circle with everyone in the room born the same month as you!"

Presentation Skills for Prosperity

To prepare for this job, I had to memorize a 2 1/2 hour script, and then I practiced it on 12 friends. It went well because they were my friends and wanted to be supportive. The problem came when I discover that my first professional speaking engagement was in New York City in front of 1400 college freshmen, who weren't in the least bit interested in meeting other strangers in the room. They were mostly 18-year-olds with ball caps on backwards and plenty of gold chains and gang tattoos. On top of that, I had barely memorized my script.

Needless to say, the first one didn't go well, and I decided I wanted to go home and quit. I literally picked up the phone to book a flight back to the west coast. Just before dialling, however, I realized I still had 11 other cities to do over the next fourteen days. All the hotels, flights, and venues were booked. I felt too guilty about putting the company in such a bad position. So, I put on my "big girl pants" and figured out how to make it work. By the 12th event, I was rocking it. I learned more in that two weeks than most people learn in three years.

So why would I choose a profession like this when I was so shy? A profession that meant I had to speak in front of thousands of my peers, many of whom were tough to persuade. Because it helped me get over my shyness and fear.

The truth is, if you can motivate inner-city 18-year-olds to play icebreaker games, you can do anything.

Presentation Skills for Prosperity

If you have a fear of public speaking or even giving 1-to-1 presentations, welcome to the human condition, most people do. However, once you get some skills and practice, that fear will diminish greatly just like it did for me.

After university, I went on to start my own company specializing in team building, presentation skills and change leadership for people. I went from doing that locally, to nationally and then internationally. Then about 15 years ago business owners started asking me to help them with their presentation skills, and that launched my coaching business and online learning programs. About half of those individuals were from network marketing and direct selling companies.

Over time there were so many people who needed help, that I couldn't assist them all myself. That's when I decided to create my flagship program called Presentation Prosperity.

That program is now also part of **The Network Marketing Leadership Academy (http://nmla.biz).** I run this academy with my partner, Dave O'Connor, who is a Mindset Expert for network marketers and business owners. This book is a sampling of what you will get in those programs.

In this book, I want to hone in on how to have presentations that not only stand out but convert leads into team members. Being a great presenter can help you fast track to a 6-to-7 figure business. You will learn the main things that my clients say made the biggest difference in the shortest amount of time. You will also learn how to avoid the common mistakes that Network Marketers make when trying to do presentations.

These skills are useful when:

- pitching your business opportunity
- introducing your products or services
- motivating and mentoring people in your company
- or even just trying to get someone out to a meeting

They will give you an instant way to have a sense of power, poise, and purpose.

Are you ready to take your business to the next level? If you are, **GREAT.** What are you waiting for? Turn the page and let's get started.

Presentation Skills for Prosperity

Chapter 2: Introduction

In our industry there is a common saying, "Facts tell, stories sell." We are in the PEOPLE business and if you want to create a business that lasts, then creating impressive presentations with stories as the main component has to be a big part of it!

An effective presentation can mean the difference between signing someone up or coming out empty handed. Most people just present the facts and then don't understand why their listener didn't join up.

Why are stories so powerful in your presentations?

Let's quickly look at five main reasons.

> **1. A good story will engage a person's head and heart** at the same time. It engages people's senses

and makes something potentially dull and boring come alive.

2. Stories bypass most people's defense systems. People let down their guard when you tell them a story. They don't feel sold to or pressured.

3. Stories are efficient. One story can cover a topic with brevity and depth and will relate to different people with different learning styles, all at the same time.

4. People remember stories. They may not remember your name, but they will remember a story you told them, even years later. This will help a person who said "no" before remember you when life circumstances change, and your network marketing company is the ideal solution.

5. Stories can create instant rapport like nothing else. People buy products and join companies in part because they like, know and trust YOU. Stories help that happen.

Different Types of Presentations

By definition, a presentation is anything that you prepare ahead of time that you use to build your business. It can be:

- a 30-second elevator speech
- a small group at your house to sample the products
- an enrollment webinar
- a training teleseminar
- a 4 minute video for your website
- speaking at your company's annual conference

The length doesn't make a difference, nor how many people you are talking too, they are all presentations, and they are all valuable to your business.

A HUGE part of being in a network marketing company is preparing for and giving presentations. You may have experience in this from other jobs, business or hobbies. If so then you can transfer your skills, but there are still new things you may need to learn about doing that in your company.

If doing presentations was NOT part of your previous life, then the sooner you learn these skills, the faster your business will grow.

Sharing Stories vs. Sharing Concepts

Have you ever had a teacher who just droned on reciting facts and you could barely keep your eyes open? Sure, we all have.

Now, what about the teacher who made learning fun? The teacher that told stories and used examples to explain facts in a way that made you want to listen all day. The teacher that you knew cared about you and wanted to help you learn. I bet you looked forward to those classes!

It's the same in your business. People are not interested in just hearing the facts and features about your business. This is a mistake many new and experienced presenters make. Say you share a fact such as "our company is in 23 countries around the world."

Most people can't translate how that might benefit them. They would need a story or example. Here's a quick tip. Anytime you share fact, or feature about your business, start a new sentence with the words "That means + a story or example". See below for a couple of examples.

> "Our company is in 23 countries around the world. That means, if you travel to other places, or have friends and family in other countries, you can grow an international business. My sister lives in Melbourne, Australia, so together we built a team there. It's been a great excuse to travel there, see them, and have income from two different economies. When the economy here went down I still had the Australia team going strong."

In short, your job is to take the complex information about your company and put it into bite size pieces that are meaningful for the individuals you talk to.
That means getting to know what IS meaningful to them. And it's going to be different for different people. Don't

assume you know what that is. Make sure you ask lots of questions and then listen. In a one-to-one, let them do a lot of the talking.

Here are a variety of reason people join network marketing businesses:
- getting out of the rat race
- having a second income
- staying home with the kids
- working with a group of like-minded people
- living a more healthy lifestyle
- having retirement income
- mentoring and helping others
- the ability to travel
- to work for a company that makes a difference in the world

When talking to people, you need to inspire them with the possibility that they could reach meaningful goals.

They also want to know that you care about them and that you understand where they are at in life.

The truth is, many people feel like those around them don't care, don't listen, are simply focused on their own needs. Most network marketing companies are structured so that the only way you can grow is if you help others grow. That's a big motivator for many people to join. Many people are stuck in a traditional company where you may need to compete AGAINST your co-workers to survive.

Make that clear in the beginning that you DO care and that you DO want them to have a more fulfilling life and then continue to let them know that. It will magnetize and encourage people who value that kind of working environment.

Now you may already be using stories, and that is great but sometimes stories can be too long winded, or they don't help you reach your business goals. Good presenters seek to distil down the essence of their stories to the universal themes that people can relate to and incorporate into their lives.

They also use a story structure that is psychologically satisfying to people. It's kind of the behind-the-scenes skills that great network marketing presenters have.

Stories are the most powerful form of self-hypnosis for better or for worse. Beneath all our limiting beliefs about ourselves is a story that is the glue holding it all together. Beneath all our empowering beliefs is also a story that takes us higher. The stories you tell others can have a powerful hypnotic effect on yourself and others to grow.

What Makes a Story Relatable?

The content of the story helps, but it doesn't always have to be something you've exactly experienced before. You just need to help people put themselves IN the story. Let's say I'm sharing about a trip I took India. Some of you may have traveled or lived there, some of you may not have. However, if I give details (sights, sounds, feelings) and talk in the present tense, it creates something called "narrative transport." This is where the listener can imagine being there. You take them there with your words. Here is an example.

> *I'm standing in front of the Taj Mahal with my two close friends. Our jaws are hanging open. It's muggy and hot, and the mist is rising from the base of the white marble dome. I can hear throngs of tourists talking in ten different languages around me. I smell Champa incense burning and feel the sun beating down on my forehead.*

See what I mean? You could almost picture yourself there.

Movies Have the Same Effect
There are certain movies that many people seem to watch over and over again. Think about that for yourself. What movies have you seen more than once?

Here is a list of the top 6:

1. Star Wars
2. Wizard of Oz
3. The Matrix
4. Gone with The Wind
5. Titanic
6. The Lion King

Why is it that people have a hunger for certain stories like this and not others? I'm sure there are movies you've seen once that you would never bother seeing again.

All of the movies you love have a certain type of structure embedded within them. It's called The Hero's Journey. *The Hero's Journey* was mapped out by myth expert, Joseph Campbell. He studied myths and stories in all cultures, throughout all times in history and found that humans basically tell the same kind of story at the very core.

For example, there is a hero or heroine who must leave their ordinary world and go on an adventure. Usually, they refuse the call to adventure at first, but often a mentor or powerful circumstance pushes through their resistance. They then face tests, enemies, obstacles and must overcome some kind of ordeal whereby they emerge a changed person. As a reward, they become stronger and grow as a person. Then they return to the ordinary world where they are now able to share their gifts with others.

Think about all your favorite heroes like Bilbo Baggins, Harry Potter, Luke Skywalker, Dorothy Gale, or Scarlett O'Hara. They went through a similar kind of journey, right? Even when short stories are told like this, they program people for good or bad. Therefore, it's very important what kinds of stories you consume and tell, because they will program you and others at a subconscious level.

Does that mean negative stories program you for negativity? Not necessarily. A good story does include challenges, conflict, and struggle. That's normal, but stories that include The Hero's Journey are powerful for personal growth and opening minds to new possibilities. That's because the structure doesn't leave the hero in darkness. The plot always includes how they transformed those obstacles and won out at the end of the day. Did you know there are Hero's Journey consultants who are hired by Hollywood writers to ensure that particular structure is included? Almost all of the top blockbuster movies have The Hero's Journey as their core structure.

Just imagine the power your personal stories when you include this structure within them. I'll show you how to tell them in a simple, short structure also known as The Ascension story.

Every good presentation should have what's called 'an ascension story.' It's an adventure you went on. It could be an inner adventure or an outer one. This may include your BIG WHY – your big mission/reason/purpose for doing your business that will inspire others. It doesn't always have to include your why, though, and you don't always have to tell a personal story. It could be someone else's story

An Ascension story is where the hero, you or someone else, faces and overcomes a challenge. It's best to have as many of these types of stories as possible.

And…

This is what the rest of this book is about. Creating presentations that inspire others to create the life of their dreams and, if appropriate, join your business or try your products and services, so that their lives will be better.

Section 1: Getting Ready For Your Presentation

Presentation Skills for Prosperity

Chapter 3: The All Important Ground Work

One thing I have learned over the years is that *PREPARATION* is the key to success in any presentation. While natural speaking ability helps, a poorly laid out presentation will undermine a great speaker. Even a great presentation given by a great presenter but to the WRONG listener will produce few results.

That's why this section of the book is the most important. In a sense you are like a farmer, all the work is done quietly, in the background for a long period of time before you see any results. You have the detail work of preparing the ground, planting the seeds, watering and weeding first. But, eventually it all pays off, and you get the harvest.

Presentation Skills for Prosperity

When it comes to creating presentations the ground work and seed planting is learning about your audience, and getting clear on your purpose for the presentation.

Then you go into brainstorm mode where you make a list of all possible stories, quotes, facts, background research, humour, and support materials you might want to add in.

Then comes the process of structuring it and creating an outline, and perhaps even scripting it where appropriate. You might even create a slideshow and prepare written material to support your presentation.

Once your presentation is all prepared it helps to memorize it; at least your opening, stories, and closing. Then you'll want to do a mental rehearsal where you imagine yourself as you present and everything going very, very well.

Harvest times comes as you stand on stage, or walk into that coffee shop and your listeners seem engaged. And even better, perhaps they decide to go on the next stage of the journey with you. That could mean just being willing to stay in touch, or come to a meeting, or try your product, or use your advice, or even sign up to be a business associate.

Celebration time!
But…

That kind of celebration is usually the result of good preparation beforehand. If you've ever listened to a presentation that was hard to follow, boring, or irrelevant to you, it's likely because the person didn't do the appropriate *preparation ahead of time*. Don't fall into that trap. Good preparation alone can skyrocket your confidence. I've seen people go from a nervous wreck to totally calm and collected just because they took the time to prepare properly.

Presentation Goals Clarity Process

As you begin, it is important to set the goals and lay the groundwork in three critical areas:

1. **Discovering Your Personal Vision**

2. **Figuring Out the Right Niche**

3. **Finding Hungry Prospects within that Niche**

This is the groundwork for the whole **Presentation Prosperity (http://nmla.biz)** system to work. The idea is to find that SWEET SPOT whereby you're finding the overlap between:

- who you are (your values, experiences, credibility, passions, skills and expertise)
- who your ideal team members are (their values, experiences, skills and needs)

- the benefits of your products, services and business opportunity.

In other words, when you complete the groundwork in these three areas you will discover your uniqueness, passion, and skills. Then, you find the communities you could tap into, what hurts them, what's changing for them, and the goals they have. Then you simply match your company benefits to their goals.

Most people in network marketing don't do this. They just take the standard company presentation and say the same thing to everyone, and so it's very hit and miss. When you do this groundwork, when you personalize it, when you start using the language that will speak directly to the needs of your particular listeners, when you have created simplicity and clarity---then magic moves in and you see results.

You will then summarize all that in your Mission Statement (which we cover later in the book).

The reason I created this years ago is that people intellectually understood the importance of sharing a compelling WHY for doing their business, but it wasn't just popping into their head. Most people need a process like this to think outside the box, to brainstorm and see connections that weren't obvious before.

Therefore, this is a practical, step-by-step process for finding your WHY or further clarifying an existing WHY and then putting it into simple language. By the way, you may have several WHYs, and your WHY may change over time. Even if you think you know it, try the process anyway. You may be surprised at what you discover.

This brainstorming process will further distil your existing WHY or help you come up with a new, compelling one if you don't have a BEFORE working with anyone on their presentation. You can have great stories, a great structure, fantastic delivery, but if the presentation doesn't come from a place of mission/vision/values and doesn't speak to your listener's needs; then it's often a waste of your time and theirs. I see too many presentations like that, and I don't want that to happen to you.
to you.

Matching your needs with your listener needs is always No 1. It's like laying a solid foundation for your presentation, and then everything else comes after that. You may already have an idea of your uniqueness, your community to serve and a great mission statement, but it's also important to revisit those things from time to time as they may change, or they may need to be further distilled.

Answering Questions About Your Life

For this next part, I highly suggest that you either have a pen and paper, computer, tablet or cell phone or whatever you feel the most comfortable taking notes. It is important to have your answers written down as you will be using them to create several types of presentations—from long ones to short ones.

Discovering Your Personal Vision

Here are three questions to answer. Write down as many answers as possible for each one.

1. What Is Unique About You?
Here are two areas to write about:

- personality traits
- circumstances in your life

Throughout this entire exercise, please make sure you list all kinds of traits. They all have a part to play in making your presentation great.

For example:
I am a good listener
I'm bad at time management
I'm very outgoing and talkative
My parents were from Croatia
I have two older sisters
I was homeschooled until I was nine years old
I am deaf in one ear
I got fired from my job last year
I once won a national essay contest

2. What Have You Learned & What Are Your Main Skills?

List your schooling, job training, street smarts, things you have learned as a student of life, and where you have the most life experience.

For example:
I have a college diploma in marketing
I worked five years as a real estate agent
I taught myself social media marketing
I can speak Croatian, Serbian, French, and English
I have been married and divorced twice
I cured myself of dyslexia
I spent three years singing in a choir
I spent seven years as a stay-at-home mom
I volunteer every year at the local jazz festival

3. What Excites You About Your Company's Products, Services and Business Opportunity?

For example:
low start cost
money back guarantee
proprietary skin cream
best super food for allergies
car bonus
incentive travel
the company is in 23 countries

Make as big a list as possible in all categories.

Choosing the Right Niche & Finding Hungry Prospects within that Niche

Here are three questions to help clarify the types of people to place your focus.

1. Communities or Niches?

What are the types of people that you would ideally like to work with, to have on your team? You can list them by a variety of criteria such as:

- the kind of work they do
- age range
- life situation
- values, activities
- geographical area

For example:

New mothers with jobs in their 30's from my hometown, who have a good work ethic

French speaking golfers who are near retirement, who love to travel

Couples in their 40's who are entrepreneurially-minded and enjoy healthy living

2. What Hurts? What Changing for Them?

Choose just ONE community to do this next exercise, otherwise, it's too difficult to complete. Keep this one group in mind and keep your company's solutions in mind, then ask yourself the following questions.

What problems do they face?
What bothers them the most?
What is changing for them?
What are their top goals right now?

For example:
> *New mothers in their 30's with jobs, from my hometown who have a good work ethic*

> What problems do they face?
>> *They don't want to go back to a job after having a baby*
>> *They are worried about having enough income*

> What bothers them the most?
>> *Having to be away from their children*
>> *Having no time freedom*
>> *Losing their competitive edge in the marketplace*

> What is changing for them?
>> *Priorities are now more focused on kids and family*
>> *Time is more precious*
>> *More health issues, lower energy than before getting pregnant*

Very few part time job opportunities in our hometown

What are their top goals right now?
Be with their children more
Still have good income
More time freedom
Stay competitive in the marketplace

3. How Can My Network Marketing Company Help Them Get Solutions?

Finally, brainstorm on all the ways that your products, services, and business opportunity can serve this community. How can your company help solve their problems and reach their goals?

Now for the moment we are going to leave these questions and your answers. Don't worry; you didn't do this work for nothing. We will be using it throughout the rest of this book to create your mission statement, create your why story and to structure your presentation to the perfect audience.

Structuring Your Presentation

Without an order leading to a specific objective, most presenters tend to go off on tangents and lose their listeners. Therefore, it is best to organize the material ahead of time rather than just "winging it."

There are two main types of presentations:

Information – Eg. How to use the company tools to measure your progress.

Persuasion – Eg. The benefits of becoming a business associate

Most persuasive talks are also informational, in that the listeners need information to be persuaded. Most network marketing and direct selling presentations have an element of both. Choose the order you think will best suit your objectives:

Problem-solution order: This method is useful for a listener who is totally new to your products, services or business opportunity. Solutions usually require expenditures of time, energy or money. Therefore, to persuade people to accept your solution, it helps to outline the problem first. For example, as we age our skin loses collagen causing your skin to droop and be more fragile. Our anti-aging products reverse that process.

List of reasons order: This method is useful for a listener that mostly buys into your idea. You can go straight to the reasons why they might want to open their minds to your idea. For example, since you already use our products and have referred them to several friends, you could sign up as an associate and receive a commission for each person that signs up.

Criteria satisfaction order: This is best used for resistant listeners.

1. This is what you say you want
2. This is how we can give you what you want
3. Here's the proof that we can give it

For example:
You say you need to bring in more income and are tired of your job. Our company offers you a way to have unlimited income, to work from home, to set your own hours and to be promoting a company that helps people have better lives.

I went from earning $50,000 per year working 10 hours a day for a company that pollutes the atmosphere. Now, I earn over $90,000 a year for a company that increases people's well-being, working when I want, with whom I want, and doing that from home.

Negative order: This is another good method for resistant audiences. The order goes something like this:

1. These are the choices you have made
2. Here is why these choices do not benefit you
3. If you go with the choice I'm suggesting, you will be much more satisfied

For example:
You want to have enough money to retire at 65. Right now, you have very little savings and only 15 years until retirement. With

your present job, you now have no extra money each month for savings and your retirement income will be, at best, poverty level.

Furthermore, last year it was reported that 50% of seniors in the US cannot financially support themselves. Your current strategy is not going to allow you to retire at 65. As a business associate with our company, you create passive income that can grow exponentially, so that you can live comfortably during your retirement years and into old age.

Timeline of a 60 Minute Presentation

Finally, as we end this chapter, I want to give you a basic outline of what a 60-minute presentation might look like.

1. Opening (2 Minutes)
2. Overview (5 Minutes)
3. Point #1 (10 Minutes)
4. Point #2 (13 Minutes)
5. Point #3 (15 Minutes)
6. Closing (15 Minutes)

This structure is just to get you started. Feel free to get creative with it, once you have some good skills.
In the rest of this section we will look at:

- Creating a Powerful Why Story,
- Creating a Short, Easy-to-Present Mission Statement
- How to Pitch Your Opportunity.

Finding Out Your Presenter Personality Style

Some people can read a book and get results, but if you are like most people, you need more.

If you're part of a network marketing company doing the D.A.N.C.E. Personality Style Quiz is very important. **http://carlarieger.com/MLMDANCEQUIZ** It will help you stop prospecting in ways that don't work for your personality style AND increase your conversions by up to 75%.

This is a personality profiling system designed to improve your conversations and presentations so you increase your rapport, referrals and income. Many people like you miss out on connecting with your listeners because of 2 reasons.

1) Your style isn't matching your listener's style
2) You're trying to be someone you're NOT

For example, have you ever found that you talk to one person and they totally "get" what you're talking about? You get along well, and they sign-up, or buy your products or services.

And then you talk to another person in exactly the same way and they just aren't interested. Of course, sometimes it's the wrong timing for them or the wrong fit, but sometimes it might just be the WAY you're communicating.

They just don't get it because it doesn't work with their learning style. If you are able to switch styles and speak their language, you would probably notice a much higher conversion rate. In the D.A.N.C.E. profiling system you'll learn about 4 basic personality styles and 1 blended one. And, most people are good at enrolling people like them, but then fall flat when it comes to enrolling the other 3 styles so that's why you could be missing out on 75% of the population.

The other problem people face is trying to use a style of marketing that doesn't work for them. For example, some people are warmhearted and natural storytellers who magnetize people to them, but they don't do so well chasing after people. As soon as they try to do that, it all falls apart.

In contrast, others aren't magnetizers, but they ARE great at outbound marketing. They are more what you might call "electric". They're great at calling, reaching out, inviting people to consider their offer…boldly going after their goals. This works for them, but not the magnetic styles of marketing.

Then there are others who are charismatic and electric marketers but if they try to be systematized or scripted, it completely throws them off.

Still a fourth type is magnetic but more in a task-oriented way. They need scripts and systems to do well. They also don't do well chasing after people but they get results by being consistent in measured ways and that magnetizes people to them.

Then there is a 5th style that's well balanced, like a chameleon who can jump back and forth between whatever style is appropriate based on the circumstances.

It would be interesting to find out which style you are, right? Get it for FREE here:
http://carlarieger.com/MLMDANCEQUIZ

Then, once you know your strengths and weaknesses you can stop trying to do marketing that doesn't work for you. Many people feel like they're hitting their head against a wall over and over again trying to follow someone else's style. As soon as they run their business in a style that works for them, poof, the magic comes in--less effort, more income and success.

Secondly, you can greatly increase your success by knowing how to assess the personality style your listeners, and matching your style to theirs. This doesn't mean being inauthentic, but being able to speak their language when necessary. It's like going to another country and learning enough of the language to get by. Now of course, some people are good at becoming fluent in many languages, and you can also learn to do that too through using the DANCE personality profiling system.

So, download this quiz and find out whether you are a:

Demonstrator
Asserter
Narrator
Contemplater
Expert

Successful network marketers and direct sellers know this secret tactic. They know how to appeal to the communication style of their listener. Now you can too. Once you get the quiz you can read about the strengths and challenges of your style, AND you'll learn about the best ways to recognize the style of your listeners so you can match it. **http://carlarieger.com/MLMDANCEQUIZ**

In the next chapter, we are going to look at the power of creating your 'Why' story and how you can use it to overcome objections and instill instant trust in your potential team members.

Presentation Skills for Prosperity

Chapter 4: Story Basics

Let's look at how you structure your story within a presentation. Warning. If you just tell the story exactly how it happened in real life, it will tend to be too long-winded, complicated, and not as likely to serve your goals.

Here you will discover a 5-part story structure that helps make stories more relatable and more psychologically satisfying to your listeners. What makes an appealing story are values that are meaningful to people, and universally applicable life lessons. In the next chapter, I will have you pick values that are important to you as the base of your story.

The Hero's Journey

How do you know when you're telling a story, as opposed to just explaining a concept? This is an important distinction that might not be obvious to people. A story is defined as having a full beginning, middle, and end, with characters, conflict, motivations, and often a moral to the story.

You can tell stories of other successful people in your company, or the story of your company's rise to success. But it's also important to tell personal stories. Why? It acts as a kind of resume for people who might want to join your business. People join, in part, because they like, know and trust YOU! Therefore, you need to give them a way to get to know your background, skills, experience, and values. If they relate to you, if they like you, then they are more likely to sign up.

Most people ask me "I can't think of anything interesting from my life to talk about." But, the truth is, there are probably a thousand stories you could be telling from your life. You are a treasure chest of interesting incidents. It all depends on how you frame those experiences.

That said, it's tricky just to come up with a story out of thin air. Have you ever had a child say "Mummy, tell me a story?" And then you draw a blank. It helps to have triggers. Here are a few. If you already have a story idea, great, use this material to build on it. If not, use these triggers to brainstorm on possible story ideas.

A challenging goal you achieved. For example:
When you overcame a financial difficulty
When you survived an accident
When did you do something daring, like skydiving
When you overcame a bad habit like worrying, or overeating

An inner dilemma you finally resolved. For example:
When you left a successful career because it wasn't right for you anymore
When you faced your fears of being an entrepreneur, so you could have a better life
When you decided to start a family
When you moved to a new country

A conflict you resolved with another person or group. For example:
When you won a court battle
When you resolved a conflict with an ex, and now you're friends
When you solved an issue on your team, and now everyone gets along

A great discovery you made. For example:
How negative emotions affect the ph balance of your body
Discovering your birth parents
Discovering how much you love public speaking

The Ascension Structure: A 5 Part Process

If you are educating your team or talking about the business opportunity, it helps to use a story structure that outlines a pathway to success. The 5 Part Ascension Story Structure works well for these kinds of 5-15 minute stories. Once you understand and use this formula, you can keep people engaged on even the driest topic.

People tend to be drawn into a story if there is a certain structure to the story, or what myth expert, Joseph Campbell, might call The Monomyth, also known as the hero's journey or ascension story. As I mentioned in previous chapters, this is a basic pattern of stories found all over the world and from all times in history that seems to have a powerful psychological effect on listeners.

Stories told exactly how they happened are generally too complicated and therefore confuse or bore an audience. Because of this, top speakers break their stories down to their essence, uncovering key universal lessons that people can apply to their own lives.

In this 5-part story structure, I've taken key principles of Joseph Campbell's Hero's Journey and applied them to a 5-10 minute teaching story format. Using this formula helps you uncover the universal truths in your stories, which in turn will help your listeners stay engaged while also learning from your message. Let's look at the five stages.

Stage 1 – Set the Platform

What's the context of the story? How does it begin? Who, what, where, when? This is like the springboard that you jump from. For example, in The Wizard of Oz, we learn that Dorothy is an orphan who lives in Kansas with her aunt and uncle. A mean lady next door wants to have her dog, Toto, put down because he gets into her garden. So, Dorothy runs away and gets caught in a storm. If you don't set the platform, if we don't know who Dorothy is, where she comes from and what's happening in her life, then the rest of the story doesn't make sense.

Stage 2 – Tilt the Platform

What is a discovery, decision, trouble, or conflict that the hero encounters? For example, Dorothy gets caught in a tornado and ends up in The Land of Oz. If you don't 'Tilt the Platform,' then the story won't engage as many people. If Dorothy just stays on the farm and nothing extraordinary happens for the whole story, few people would continue to watch the movie.

Stage 3 – Consequences

What happens as a result of the platform tilt? This is often the bulk of the story. For example, Dorothy meets munchkins, witches, scarecrows, and wizards. If you don't spell out the consequences of a platform tilt, your listener will get frustrated. For example, if you take Dorothy from Kansas and drop her in the Land of Oz, then end the story, people are going to wonder what happened next. It creates an unresolved loop in a person's mind.

Some writers do it on purpose. It's called a 'cliffhanger' when a TV show writer does it at the end of an episode to ensure you tune in next week. Novelists use it to ensure you keep going through the chapters. You become driven by your curiosity to find out how the main character resolves the platform tilt.

Stage 4 – Getting Back to Stability

How does the main character get back to stability? For example, Dorothy must kill the witch, bring back her broom to the wizard to get home. And in the end, she just needs to click her ruby slippers three times, and that's what gets her home. If you don't get the main character back to stability, if the character doesn't achieve their goal, then your story can become a tragedy or a "slice of life" story. That's an artistic choice that many a story writer makes. However, if you want your business story to open people's minds to your products or opportunity, then it helps to include this stage 4. For example, if Dorothy goes through all her adventures in Oz but never gets back home, it doesn't teach the listener anything about how to get over challenges.

Feel good stories, teaching stories and comedies always resolve the dilemma and bring the main character back to wholeness. If you want to teach or inspire people with your stories, this is often a better way to end your story, unless you want to tell a cautionary tale such as what can happen if you drink and drive.

Stage 5 – New Platform

Conventional stories rarely state the point of the story or describe how the main character changes. That is best left to each listener individually. However, in The Wizard of Oz, there is a moment in the end when Dorothy wakes up in her bedroom. She's been unconscious due to a concussion. Her loved ones are around her and she says "There's no place like home." It's a "Coming of Age" story where Dorothy goes from feeling discontent about her home and life, to feeling appreciative for it by the end. It's a journey of soul maturity.

As an educator, you may want to ensure your point is made by adding stage 5 and expressing the reason why you told the story and explore what people might gain from listening to it.

In the next chapter, we will be looking at the power of creating your "why" story and how you can use it to overcome objections and instill trust in your potential team members.

Presentation Skills for Prosperity

Chapter 5: The Power of Creating Your Why Story

Have you ever listened to a presentation where you just heard facts? For example, our company is in 23 countries. Our flagship product is made with only organic ingredients. Then, at the end, you think, "They still haven't told me WHY I should join this company or use this product."

Yes, people do require some of the facts to make an intelligent decision. However, first, you need to tell them how it solves a problem they have or helps them reach an important goal. For example, if your prospect's problem is that she's seeing too many lines on her face, she needs to see a before and after image of a woman on the skin care program. If your prospect's goal is to be at home more with her kids, then she needs to see an example of a working mum who gave up her job and now makes enough doing this business from home.

Sometimes the presentation provided by your company will help you do this, but too often it doesn't. Put yourself in your prospect's shoes. Ultimately they want to be inspired, to know that their needs and their dreams can be fulfilled. They want to know WHY they should join your team, or use your product. That is what your 'WHY story' does, or the 'WHY story' of someone else in your company that you have permission to use. Why you use these products over other similar products in the marketplace. Why you chose this home based business over all the other ones.

Stories are like the element of fire. They can warm up connections between you and your listeners. They can ignite motivation, and melt away resistance. On the flip side, they can also burn and destroy. For example, character assassinations, war propaganda stories, or disempowering stories you tell about yourself. So make sure you tell empowering stories that leave people better than how you found them. This will open them up to new possibilities.

Now you may be thinking to yourself, but my 'Why Story' isn't great, it isn't inspiring enough. The product didn't cure a rare disease, or I haven't made a huge sum of money, yet. Firstly, you just need to change your perception on what makes for a great WHY story. Secondly, you would be amazed at how powerful a simple experience can be for your listeners. They want to hear stories of people that are like them; who are accomplishing things that they can maybe see themselves doing. Your simple WHY story makes that happen.

I'll give you an example of how I came to find one of my WHY stories because it might give you ideas about how simple it can be for you.

My WHY Story

In the early days of my career as a speaker and trainer, I was doing ok, but my growth was slow.

At the time, I was focused on presenting Fun as a Team Building Tool. It was the idea that "groups that play together stay together." There were lots of stats that a fun team meant more motivation, higher sales and stayed healthier. Maybe you've noticed that on your MLM team. If the energy in your team is good it does help sales and helps attract good people. The opposite is also true. If the energy on your team is not good, it can negatively affect sales, and make good people leave. Some teams naturally have a sense of joy and camaraderie, but some don't.

I started getting hired to lead groups through all kinds of fun teambuilding activities, to teach them how to marry work and play. At the time, I never thought to include a personal story. People liked my programs, but my career had levelled out.

Then one day after a presentation in Savannah Georgia, the organizer took me out for dinner. Her name was Mary Beth Wilson. I had just spent the day with her group doing teambuilding. I was also telling them about the idea of marrying work and play, of not treating your work like drudgery, but instead to find joy throughout the day to keep your energy up.

She loved the day and so off we went to sit in a restaurant in one of those old southern mansions with the white pillars and the Spanish moss hanging from the oak trees. We are having our Mint Juleps on the veranda. A fan is blowing warm air onto us. It is a hot, muggy evening and the sun is setting.

With a warm smile Mary Beth sips her Mint Julep and says in her Southern drawl, "Just curious, why do you teach people to have more fun while working? It's such an unusual profession."

I paused. I was taken aback by her question. Finally, I said: "I don't know. I never really thought about WHY before." She sat there will this inquisitive smile so that I could search through the back story of my life to find a reason. Then something occurred to me. "Maybe because I came from the 'overly serious' family. And I'm being a *rebel*."

She says, "Tell me more."

So I told her about my background. My family was hard-core serious, solemn, linear, logical, academic, achievement-oriented people who were immigrants. My mother was British and as a young woman ran off to Canada where she met and married my father, who was

Presentation Skills for Prosperity

Austrian. My parents not only didn't value fun, playfulness and humor, they didn't get it.

I remember as a kid; I'm ten years old. We're around the dinner table. I heard something at school that day, so I say,

"Mom, why don't cannibals like to eat clowns?"

My mother is looking down at her plate cutting her broccoli spear and responds in her upper-class British accent, "I don't know, dear, why?"

"Because they taste funny."

My mother pauses to reflect on my answer with a puzzled look on her face. "That doesn't make any sense dear."

I was about to try and explain the joke, but she continued. "Clowns don't normally frequent the jungles of Africa where cannibals can be found. Just be quiet and eat your broccoli."

Now, don't get me wrong. I loved my mom and admired her. She believed it was her duty to help make the world a better place, like helping set up community support for women and children in poverty. She just did it with a solemnity that she thought was befitting of the job. So, I grew up, and I followed in her footsteps. I became very serious, worried all the time, goal oriented, academic and diligent in wanting to struggle and work hard to make the world a better place. Seven years of post-secondary education, three part-time jobs all the way through and at a certain point in my early twenties it all fell apart.

I am in a public speaking training program. Yes, I did not burst from the womb as a natural public speaker. When I first started out, I was bad, just like most people who start. I am standing on a stage in front of 65 people practicing my speech for the class. The leader is a woman from the Bronx sitting in the back row. She is studying me inquisitively. I stop and looked up. She is shaking her head and smiling. "How old are you?"

"I'm 23, why?"

With a Cheshire grin on her face, she says, "Cause you act like a 45-year-old insurance underwriter."

I didn't know what an insurance underwriter was, but I knew it wasn't good when it comes to public speaking.

She continued, "You're so serious. You're young, try having more fun when you speak. If you're this serious now then what are you going to be like in 20 years? Lighten up already. Get off the stage."

I got off the stage that day confused and embarrassed. I'm driving home and I am thinking, maybe she is right, I AM overly serious. I'd wake up every morning and go for a five-mile run, pump iron, then eat my quarter cup of low-fat yogurt and my one celery stick. My wardrobe consisted of colors such as taupe, charcoal, and pewter. My idea of fun on the weekend was highlighting my dog-eared copy of Plato's Republic.

I thought I've got to change. So I took this elective at university – which was a comedy improvisation acting course. Maybe you've seen the TV show, *Whose Line is it Anyways*? It's basically a series of games or "handles" that you play with a group of other actors. You have no script, and the idea is to be as funny as possible. I wasn't very good at first, in fact, I sucked completely, but I had to keep getting up every week and falling on my face.

And, like anything you do for long enough, I started to develop some skills. And that's when I got hooked. Many people who do improv classes tend to get hooked because you need to be very present in the moment, and that gives you a kind of euphoria. I took more Improve classes. Then, I signed up for clowning, comedy writing, cartooning, and even did stand-up comedy classes. I worked HARD at comedy because that was my thing. I even went on to have my own comedy troupe and we performed at festivals.

Thankfully, over time I developed a much more fun-loving, celebratory, light-hearted personality as my teacher had suggested I do. And now decades later, I'm actually younger at heart than I was back at 23. I'm more easy-going and less stressed. I'm more compassionate with myself and others, and less judgmental. I wear more colorful clothes. And best of all, I'm more popular. There's an old saying "Lighten up and your network will grow because people get attracted by the light."

I finish telling all the above to Mary Beth and she takes it all in. Takes another sip of her Mint Julep, pats the edge of her mouth with a hanky and then asks, "That makes complete sense. And I also sense there's something more. A bigger, deeper reason. Am I right?"

I'm thinking to myself, what's with all the questions? But, the truth is, one of the best ways to find your WHY is to sit around with a friend and ask each other "Why do you do what you do?" Do it over and over again until you get down to the core, if possible. That's what happened to me that day. I suddenly remembered a deeper WHY. Sometimes your REAL WHY is something you forgot until you are prompted to remember. But, I was uncomfortable to share it with her because it was quite vulnerable. I'll tell you what is was….later on.

As you can see, you don't have to have a superhero story; you just need to have experienced something that will be relatable to others.

Creating Your Why Story

The great thing about WHY stories is that you can use them in so many different situations. You can create a:

✓ Product Testimonial Story
✓ Why You Joined Your Company Story
✓ How You Achieved Your Recent Success Story
✓ A Training Story (E.g. Using social media)

As you are thinking about creating your next story (or maybe your FIRST story), you need to ask yourself, "What type of story do I want to create first?"

Now if you are like me, you learn better when you have an example to follow. So as we go through the questions below, I am going to give you an example. I will share how a client of mine, Rita, filled in her answers, so you can see how it is done. She chose to do a story on a flagship product sold by her company, which was a wonderful superfood drink.

> **1. Who are your listeners?** In Rita's case, it was potential customers. Now the more specific you can get, the easier it will be to choose a story. She focused her story on new mothers or parents. In other words, people like her. Why do this? Because you will better understand how to tell the story in a way that it will be interesting to them.
>
> **2. Where will you be telling the story?** For her, it would be in a home gathering or one-to-one on the phone. Even though one-to-one's are usually a conversation, it's important to sprinkle a few stories and examples into the conversation so that people "get it" quicker.
>
> **3. What are the outcomes you would like from telling your story?** Rita wasn't trying to get people to join her business yet. She just wanted them to get

familiar with the product and start to use it regularly. Most people who joined her business had become customers first.

4. What's in it for them to listen? For this one you have to step into their shoes. Rita knew that this product helps increase energy, lessen joint pain, improve skin, memory, mood and lose weight. Those are things lots of new mothers want, right? Now the other great thing about stories is that you aren't necessarily telling them that they will experience these benefits because you can get in trouble for making those kinds of claims. Instead, you tell them your experience, and they can decide for themselves if they'd like to try it based on your experience.

Your Values

What are the core values of the story? Values help people connect emotionally to you and your story. This also helps magnetize the right kind of people who share the same kind of values as you, which may be important for longevity on your team.

Take a look at this list below and choose ten values that relate most to the questions you just answered on the previous page.

Presentation Skills for Prosperity

accuracy	elegance	love	rapport
achievement	emotional well being	learning	recreation
acknowledgment	empowerment	leadership	refinement
adventure	excellence	loyalty	resoluteness
aesthetics/beauty	excitement		respect
altruism		magic/magnetism	reliability
ambition	humility/humbleness	making a difference	resilience
appreciation	independence	mindset mastery	reward &
assertiveness	integrity	meaning	recognition
attentiveness	intelligence	moderation	risk-taking
authenticity		motivation	right attitude
autonomy	financial abundance		romance
	focus	nature	
balance	free spirit	natural healing	sacredness
boldness	freedom	nurturing	security
	fun		serenity
caring		openness	solitude
charity	gentleness	orderliness	self-expression
clarity	going with the flow	originality	self esteem
collaboration	grace	patience	self realization
commitment	gratitude	participation	sovereignty
community		partnership	service
compassion	health	passion	spirituality
commitment	holistic	peacefulness	success
communication	honesty	performance	support
confidence	honor	personal growth	
connection	humor	personal power	trust
contribution		persistence	tradition
creativity	independence	power	tranquility
	intention	poise	
devotion	intuition	privacy	vitality
directness	inventiveness	productivity	visionary thinking
discipline		professionalism	
diplomacy	joy	prosperity	wildness
daring		purposeful life	willingness
dynamic	kindness		wonder
			worthiness

Regarding the superfood drink, Rita chose these words:

1. empowerment
2. health
3. holistic
4. joy

5. natural healing
6. nurturing
7. right attitude
8. vitality
9. energy
10. creativity

What ten words come to mind for you?

Feel free to add a word that you don't see there.

Then, once you have your ten, see if you can get that down to your top three. In Rita's case, they were:

1. natural healing
2. joy
3. vitality

What top three words come to mind for you?

These will be the lens through which you tell your story.

Story Triggers

Next, you want to look at story triggers. Now you may already have a story in mind. If so, that's great. If you don't, these story triggers can help. You want to be thinking about a story that will meet your story goal from the four questions you answered and that will embody the top three values you chose.

Presentation Skills for Prosperity

As we talked about earlier, here are five types of circumstances in life that tend to create good stories.

1. What is a challenge you overcame?
2. What is a decision that changed your life?
3. What is a discovery that changed your life?
4. What is an accident or loss that you learn from?
5. What is trouble you got into, that you managed to turn around?

Pick stories with happy endings because these tend to empower others. You don't want to be telling discouraging stories or where you are still in the middle of sorting it all out.

Here are examples from my life that I turned into a story:

1. **Challenge** – how I got over dyslexia
2. **Decision** – how I decided to be less serious and more light-hearted
3. **Discovery** – how I discovered public speaking as a career
4. **Accident/Loss** – how losing my first job led me to start my own business
5. **Trouble** – how my worst speaking engagement taught me my best skills

You can also pick stories from anytime in your life from childhood right up to the present. It helps to go through your life in 10-year increments and see what comes up.

Take a few moments right now and make a list of as many stories as you can. I'll be here when you get back... Finished? Great.

Now let's take a look at what Rita chose. After an exhaustive list, she picked how she lost her baby weight because that's a popular topic with her "new mom" listeners. Do you see how answering your four questions, knowing your audience, and knowing your values leads more clearly to choosing the right story?

Structuring Your Story

Now this is where The Hero's Journey we talked about in the last chapter comes in. You are going to take all that you have just done and compile it into your WHY story. Are you excited? You should be. This is a powerful tool that is going to take you to the next level in your business. So, let's fill in each part.

Working Title: _____

Opening (enhance listener curiosity): Question, memorable fact about yourself, a startling statistic, challenges or goals you can help them with. E.g. *Here's an example from my life that might help you find your WHY story.*

Part 1 - Set the platform: Where does this story begin? What time in history? What do people need to know (facts, circumstances, context) that will help people understand the message? Hint: it should be in contrast to #2 below. E.g.

In the early days of my career, I was doing ok, but my growth was slow.

Part 2 - Tilt the platform: What is the new element that changed things? (challenge, decision, conflict, discovery, trouble, new direction). E.g. *The organizer of my event asked me why I did the kind of work I do.*

Part 3 - Consequences: What happened as a result of this tilt or change? Who and what got impacted? What kind of chaos did it create? How were you emotionally, mentally, physically, or spiritually affected? What circumstances were now different? This will be the bulk of your story. E.g. *I talked about my childhood and young adulthood and found incidents that helped form my values and decisions around marry work and play.*

Part 4 - Getting back to Stability: What is the transforming idea that got you back to some sort of stability? What helped you recover? E.g. Perspective shift, asking for help, getting help from an unexpected source, being patient, doing something different, etc. E.g. *My teacher told me I was too serious and should go learn how to lighten up.*

Part 5 - New status quo: What does it all mean? What values are at the core of the story? What did you learn? What is the core universal wisdom this story illustrates? Hint: this is the place to include your "why" or mission statement. E.g. *I learned that lightening up made me less stressed, more compassionate, and happier.*

Call to Action: This is where you want to now invite your listener to take an action that would lead to a solution they are looking for. E.g. *Re-discovering how to be more light-hearted tends to have multiple benefits in terms of life and business growth.*

Congratulations, you have the basis of a great story. Now is the time to write it out. You can do it free hand. If so, just do it double-spaced to give you room to change things. Or do it on the computer. Every 750 words you write is approximately five minutes of talk.

Rita's Story

Let's take a look at how Rita's story all came together. You'll see the different parts of the story as we shift from one to the other, so you better understand the structure.

[Opening - Enhancing listener curiosity] Have you ever heard yourself say I don't remember being this tired when I was younger? Or my joints ache so much more often? Or my favorite, I can't seem to remember things like I used to? Does anyone experience any of those things? Great.

[Setting the platform] That's what I heard myself saying over and over again last year after my baby was born. At the same time, my new baby had lots of health problems. She had a skin rash all over her body, and so I went to medical doctors, but they couldn't help me. I went to a naturopath, nothing. Homeopath. Nutritionist. Nothing.

The doctor said she would grow out of it but she just wasn't, and I was still uncomfortable with my body weight.

[Tilting the platform-shift to present tense] Around that time my friend asks me to come over to her house for a small group gathering of new mothers. She wants to introduce us to a product that has been helpful for her heath and her baby.

[Normalizing common resistance] I agree to come, but inside I'm thinking, "Oh, no this is probably going to be one of those pyramid things. One more supplement that isn't going to work." But I show up, just to be polite.

After the presentation, she invites me to take the superfood drink home. Now I am nervous at first because, what if it gives me some weird side effects? But I am desperate for something that will help, so I take it.

[Consequences] I thank her, and I leave. I wake up the next morning, take some of the product, and within 15 minutes I feel like I want to go for a run. I haven't felt like that since getting pregnant.

It's 5:30 in the morning, I'm out there and feeling that early morning sun on my face, smelling the fresh dewy grass, feeling lightness in my body as I run through the park. Usually, I'm sleep deprived because I get up through the night feeding my baby but for some reason it's not bothering me today. I'm just gliding along and I'm starting to wonder if there's something illegal in this stuff. But I go running each morning that whole week. I'm so amazed.

The other thing is that my knees don't hurt the next day. And, my husband is noticing I'm not saying things like *where's my keys, honey*? I'm remembering things. The best part is that the rash on my baby's skin is going down. She isn't crying. She's obviously getting the health benefits through my breast milk.

Then after a week, I run out of the product. I don't have time to get more so I just keep going as usual. Now, however, I'm struggling to get up in the morning. I can't run for as long. I'm tired. My knees are killing me again. The baby's rash is coming back.

[Getting back to stability-highlighting the details of your solution] That's when I get online and do my research. I find out it's an all-natural superfood drink, no chemicals. It's based on $10 million worth of research. They use the latest technology to grow and harvest the plant. At that point, I run over to my friend's place and pick up as much as I can and stay on it for the next few months.

Once I am back on it, my energy comes back. My baby's health issues all clear up but I'm not totally convinced yet. Maybe it's just the placebo effect. I just THINK it should be working, so it is. That's when I tried on my 13 year old dog who's got arthritis. I put it in the dog water and he's starts walking much better and more smoothly after a few days. You can't placebo an animal or a baby for that matter. So that was it. I was hooked. Now my whole family takes it religiously.

[New status quo] Because I'm more active, my metabolism has gone back up. My figure is back to what it was before I had my baby. Yes! It's brought a lot of joy and vitality into my life and helped my family and my pets feel better. The good part for me is that this company gives me commission for everyone I sign up. I essentially get my products for free and I'm helping people have a better life. And if you want to try this product and see that works for you, just come over and talk to me. I've got samples you can try.

That's about 750 words. Rita has used that 5 minute story in a variety of places such as:

- at monthly meetings when she is asked to share a testimonial story
- during a conversation with a neighbour
- when she is doing home parties
- at networking events
- as part of a longer business presentation online
- written out on her website

And you can do that, too. That's why it's worth putting the time and effort into your story at the beginning because it can pay off for years. She basically has this story memorized, because she wordsmithed it to take out anything unimportant to the purpose of the story. If you don't do that often a story will be too long winded and people won't understand the point you're trying to make.

Rita tells the story the same way almost every time so she doesn't end up saying "um and ah" and wonder what to say next. Her strong delivery instills confidence in her listeners, and that makes them take notice and try the product for themselves.

What's Next?

Write out your whole story. It's doesn't have to be perfect, in fact, it won't. The first few times you write it out, or tell it, chances are it will have problems. That's ok. That's normal. What many people do is tell a story about why they joined the business, but they haven't thought it through and it falls flat. Then they think – I'm bad at storytelling or I'm bad at giving presentations. If you expect perfection right from the start, you will block your ability to achieve. Allow yourself the time and space to make mistakes, learn from them, and get better as you go.

You will make mistakes while you learn. Just re-write it several times and practice it a lot so that you get through the learning curve more quickly, then you will start to see results. Practice at first with people you trust, who will give you constructive feedback and not biting criticism. Say it until it becomes a part of who you are. When you have that story in place, watch out because the results will be amazing.

In Chapter 6 we are going to look at two other types of presentations you can create, that will help you get more customers and team members.

Presentation Skills for Prosperity

Chapter 6: Two Short Presentations Every Network Marketer Needs

Kim stood there hoping that the extreme nervousness she was feeling wouldn't show through. For the first time, she was using a script that she had mostly memorized. She was going to try it on a stranger she had just met at a networking event.

Now you may be thinking what's the big deal? For Kim it was. She'd had two years of trying to recruit people with little success. She had wanted to quit many times, but something inside kept her going. She intuitively knew that the answer on how to enroll people would COME, and now it finally had!

She had found the training she needed to create simple presentations that would appeal to her prospects, and now was the time to use it. Would she succeed? Find out in a later chapter how Kim went from nervous and awkward to being a top notch professional networker a lot quicker than she ever dreamed possible.

Your Mission Statement

A mission statement is a short 30 second to 1 minute presentation that has two goals. The first one is for you alone. Your mission statement helps to keep you focused on the vision and not on the obstacles. It's about what is really important to you. It helps you clarify who you are looking for regarding a new customer or team member. It clarifies your goals so that you can create effective presentations around it, so that you don't look in the wrong direction. Once you have it finished, you need to memorize it and place it all around your house as a daily reminder.

The second goal is for other people. It's for when they ask you, "So, what do you do?" Because you have already thought through the statement, wordsmithed it just right, and hopefully memorized it, you'll be able to say it with confidence and that question will never catch you off guard again. Not only does it answer the question, but it is a quick, effective commercial that will instill interest and cause the right person to ask further questions.

Creating Your Mission Statement

So for this next part, you are going to use the answers to questions I gave you in chapter 3. You thought I had forgotten about them, didn't you? I will give you the template, then show you some examples from my clients. You want to think of your ideal customer/team member and write down your mission statement geared to them.

It's not about creating something for everyone. It's about targeting down to a specific group of people that you can work well with.

My passion is to use my (insert something unique about yourself)
to help (the community you chose)
deal with/have (insert what is hurting or changing for them).
I will do this by (insert how you will connect with people,
where I will (insert how people can benefit)
so that (insert what excites you about your company).

Here are three examples:

> *My passion is to use my* leadership and fun-loving nature
> *to help* people wanting to leave the construction industry
> *deal with* their exhaustion and high overhead.
> *I will do this by* having small home parties
> *where I will* show them how to have a passive income business
> *so that* they get good health products and the retirement of their dreams.

My passion is to *use my team building training and networking skills*
to help *young working mothers*
have *an opportunity to work from home while also being part of a dynamic, fun team.*
I will do this by *hosting networking events*
where I will *show them how they can earn income and stay at home with their kids*
so that *they can have the lifestyle they choose and be part of a fun, new community of like-minded people*

My passion is to *use my experience in the performing arts*
to help *people in my small town deal with the lack of good jobs here and*
have *a good income without moving.*
I will do this by *offering creative presentations that open people's minds to our opportunity*
so that *we have a creative outlet together and a way that keeps our community together, while also providing for our families.*

Pitching A Network Marketing Business Opportunity

Just before we get into the template, here is a very important concept that you need to use when creating any presentation. It's about Left Brain/Right Brain Dominance.

That way you can ensure your presenting style appeals to both types of people.

When looking at brain dominance, some people are more left brain dominant and some are more right brain dominant. Left brain dominant people think in logical, sequential, rational, analytical, and objective ways.

Right brained people tend to think in more random, intuitive, holistic, subjective, synthesizing kinds of ways. But, of course, we all use both sides of the brain all the time, it's just that some people lead with their left brain and other people lead with the right brain.

Now this is a very simplistic view of the brain, but it will serve our purposes for understanding how different people will be viewing your information or your training sessions. And since it's about 50-50 in the general population, you need to include both left brain and right brain ways of sharing information.

Left Brain

When you are creating a presentation for those who are left brained you include things like:

- **Concepts, benefits, features or theories** E.g. A home based business can mean tax savings.

- **Facts** E.g. According to a study done in 2013, the Direct Selling industry earned $178 billion US dollars worldwide.

- **Statistics** E.g. People who rate highly for happiness on psychological tests develop about 50% more antibodies when dealing with the flu virus.

- **Provocative Questions** E.g. If you don't change anything about your life now, where will you be financially in five years?

- **Quizzes or polls** E.g. The Brain Dominance Quiz below.

- **Challenges/invitations** E.g. If you spent 10 hours a week reaching out to qualified prospects I bet you could double your income in three months, who is willing to try that? Prizes are involved!

- **Logical arguments** E.g. For every one thing in your life that seems to be going wrong, chances are there are 1000 things going right.

- **Re-stating** E.g. Another way of putting it is—most people tend to focus too much on what's going wrong in life and forget to be grateful for all the wonderful things happening.

- **Summarizing** E.g. To summarize what I'm saying here, it is important that you present material in a variety of modalities that are interesting and digestible for people.

Right Brain

Now for people who tend to think in their right brain you need presentations that include:

Presentation Skills for Prosperity

- **Comparisons** E.g. People who include specific examples tend to be better presenters than those who don't.

- **Contrasts** E.g. Our network marketing company is 10x the size of our closest competitor. Examples. One benefit of joining a network marketing company is the chance to earn residual income. For example, $___ extra a month if you maintain ___ credits.

- **Quotations** E.g. "Vision is the art of seeing what is invisible to others." Jonathan Swift
- **Poems** E.g. "Above the mountains, the geese turn into the light again, painting their black silhouettes on an open sky. Sometimes everything has to be inscribed across the heavens, so you can find the one line already written inside you. - The Journey, by David Whyte

- **Humorous anecdotes** E.g. A doctor friend told me this story about her four-year-old daughter. On the way to preschool, her stethoscope was on the car seat, and her little girl picked it up and began playing with it. My friend started thinking 'my daughter wants to follow in my footsteps!' Then the child spoke into the instrument: "Welcome to McDonald's. May I take your order?"
- **Metaphors** E.g. "Don't shoot the messenger," or "All the world's a stage, and all the men and women are merely players." - Shakespeare

- **Stories** E.g. "One thing I've loved about being part of my company is…" (add details)

Business Opportunity Example

This example includes elements that will appeal to both brain dominances. This is actually a video script that one of my coaching clients put on her personalized website for her company. She also posted it on social media. Then she just adapted it for 1-to-1 conversations and business presentations.

You can use this example to create your own video script, or take pieces of it to improve one that you already have. This one is four minutes long and approximately 600 words.

> **[provocative question]** Are you at a crossroads in your life since having children? **[example]** That happened to me when I had my first child. I thought I could start a family, keep my intense job AND stay sane and fashionably attractive all at the same time. Was I ever wrong.
>
> **[quotation]** There's an old quote "I try to take one day at a time, but sometimes several days attack me at once." If that's YOU, and you're looking for a new solution, this may be of interest. I found something that is letting me be home with my kids much more often while still making a good living AND getting my figure and fashion back where it once was.
>
> **[invitation]** I invite you to listen for just 3 minutes and see if it resonates.

Presentation Skills for Prosperity

[story] Hi, I'm Leslie Miller, mother of two children, and I used to work as part of an event management team in a hotel. I loved the people and using my creativity to overcome challenges. But it was long hours, often on weekends and evenings. I was at a crossroads once the kids came along. I didn't want to give up the income, the people, or my career progression, but something had to give as my home life, and health was suffering.

A friend introduced me to this product _____ that I really loved that helps with _____. So I started telling everyone about it. She mentioned that I could make income through this company by referring it, and I could do the business from home. I declined at first because I was so busy with my job and family. Over the next six months, however, I watched her go from making a few hundred each month to several thousand. She didn't have to commute, she set her own hours and was starting to make more than I was at my job!

It is a network marketing company called _____. **[theory]** Now I'd heard some not-so-great-things about the network marketing industry. But rather than believe everything I heard, I decided to do research. **[statistic]** I discovered that the network marketing industry has grown by 90% over the last 40 years. In fact, it's one of the fastest growing industries in the world. **[fact]** Companies all over the world are switching to this model of doing business because the old model of advertising isn't working anymore. I discovered that her company was one of the top 50 in the world in its industry. **[fact]** And that there were over 8 million distributors in over 90 countries around the world. I was impressed.

[normalize common objections to MLM] But that wasn't enough for me. I'm very picky when it comes to what I get involved with and what I am willing to recommend to others. I've been burned before, and I didn't want that to happen again.

So, I researched the leadership, the compensation plan, the risks involved, the training and support offered, the quality of the products and **[comparison]** compared it with several other similar companies. This one came out ahead by a mile.

Then my friend asked me a question. If you continue on the same path for the next five years, where will you be in terms of your life goals? **[logical argument]** For me, the answer was, I would be **[metaphor]** like a petrified tree, I would still be in debt, having missed my children growing up, I would be burned out, and resentful of my life. I really didn't want that to happen. Think about that for yourself. **[provocative question]** Where will you be in five years terms of your life goals if you continue on the same path?

Presentation Skills for Prosperity

> **[summary]** Fast forward 14 months, and I'm overjoyed that I made the leap from my job to _____. **[challenge/invitation]** If this peaks your interest, I invite you to click on the link below and we'll talk and see if it's a good fit. Or, at least sign up for my newsletter. You'll get a free Self Assessment Worksheet to see if you have the aptitude to run your own home-based busines. Again, I'm Leslie Miller, thank you for listening.

For every 100 people that watched her video, 16 signed up for newsletter, and 4 booked an appointment with her. And out of those 4, often 1 buys the starter pack for her company. The video runs 24/7 and does a lot of the work for her. People who sign up on her list continue to get small offers and information about the company, and get invited again to interview with her.

Try a video script yourself, and you'll discover that you can re-purpose it in many ways, and it can be magnetizing ideal people while you sleep!

Now in section two, we will look at all the things that go into delivering a good presentation and how to overcome things like stage fright or nervousness. WAIT! I didn't forget about the rest of Kim's story. It has a really happy ending. That day she did talk to the lady at the networking event and even though she didn't join the company she did become a great customer for Kim.

That experience gave Kim the courage to keep trying. She became more and more confident with practice, and then she realized it was just a numbers game. She measured her success. For every 25 people she connected with, approximately five would become customers and one would join the business. That way she could calculate how quickly she could grow her team. It helped her know exactly what to do every day to keep her business moving forward. Now, she's making a good income and has reached a level of success in her business that she once only dreamed about. Like everyone else, she has had her ups and downs, but now that she has the skills she needs, and she has the inner knowing that nothing can stop her from reaching her goals and dreams.

Section 2:
Presentation Time

Chapter 7: How to Avoid the Top 4 Mistakes Presenters Make

First of all, I want to congratulate you on making it this far. It takes a lot of courage to take that big step and learn how to present effectively to build your business. Most people won't do it and therefore, will never see the results that you will. Over 95% of people won't even get as far as you have come now, so be proud of yourself. You've earned it.

Even top presenters make these four mistakes more often than you think. You'll discover tips to help you avoid those mistakes so that you can come across as a pro much more quickly. A really well-done presentation will just make your efforts to grow your business more efficient. If you present well the first time and even if they say "no" for now, you planted a seed that could turn into a "yes" later on. On the other hand, if you do a poor presentation, it's more likely to be a "no, forever."

Mistake #1 - Not Caring About Your Audience

Another way of saying this is, being disconnected from your listeners. It is so easy to get absorbed in how you look, trying to remember what to say, checking your text messages, or being afraid to look people in the eyes.

I'm sure you've listened to presenters like this. They're talking, but they're not really "there." They look like they're in the back of their head trying to ensure they cover the material correctly, or they are trembling with nerves.

Answer this question. Think of the last time you gave a presentation. It could be one-to-one or to a group. Remember when that was? Now, on a scale of 1 to 5, how well do you feel you were connected to and caring about your listener as you presented? 1 is very low and 5 is very high.

Cavett Robert, the great founder of the National Speakers Association said, "They don't care how much you know until they know how much you care."

That's something people pick up on right away. They know instantly, if you are there to help them or if you are there to get something from them. If you do nothing else as a presenter than care about your listener, you'll really rise above the crowd. Most people are too self-absorbed when they present. And you can make that switch in an instant. Even if you don't have all of your words perfect and you haven't had massive success yet in your business, you will really make a difference for people by being there with them.

Here's an example that my partner, Dave O'Connor, gives. He had recently been fired from his job, and his life was looking bleak when he got asked to speak at an event.

Dave's Story

I got fired from a job I'd been in for many years. In retrospect, it was a good thing, but it didn't always feel like that at the time. After quite a time wallowing in self-pity, I got this phone call out of the blue from an old friend. This woman had a yoga group, and she wanted me to talk about the power of the unconscious mind. The reason she asked me to speak on this topic was she had heard me do presentations on this before as part of my former job, and she loved what I had to say. As I always had this vision of me speaking and coaching people all over the world, this then initiated a Civil War inside of me. One part of me felt it was possible, I can do this, I was meant to do this. But another part, a far greater part of me, kept squashing the idea. It was like this voice was saying, "Who do you think you are? What do you have to offer?"

Presentation Skills for Prosperity

Isn't it ironic that when I was at my lowest point ever, I got this phone call? I usually had resistance to seizing these kinds of opportunities. In the past, however, when I could move through that resistance I always seemed to break through to a higher level of functioning in my life. It was almost like the universe was testing me, to see what I was made of, to test my commitment to my vision. In remembering that, I chose to then focus my attention on my vision, instead of my fear. Somehow I knew that despite all my uncertainty, that this was something I was meant to do.

I arrive at this venue with 500 people in the audience. I'd never spoken to more than 50 people at one time. The atmosphere is electric, and I am absolutely terrified. There I am in the restroom trying to get myself in the right frame of mine, but I am unable to shake off the doubts. My heart is beating loudly in my chest; my mouth is dry. I'm sweating profusely. I come out, and I say to the organizer, "I don't think I can do this."

She says, "Too late, Dave, you're on." I am in the wings, and I can hear the MC say, "Okay, we have a surprise guest this evening. Kate has invited this amazing speaker, and you are going to love this guy. He's going to inspire you, he's going to motivate you, he's going to blow your mind with the information that he brings you here tonight!"

Meanwhile, I am just dying inside. I am thinking – "This is going to be the worst disaster ever!" And I hear that voice of doubt, "Who do you think you are for people to listen to you and hear advice from you?"

"Ladies and gentlemen, please put your hands together for, Mr. Dave O'Connor!

The organizer leans forward and whispers in my ear, *"Dave you can do this, you were born to do this, you're going to be great."* It's times like this you need someone who believes in you more than you believe in yourself, right?

As I step out on stage, I feel these hot lights beating down on me. You can hear a pin drop in the room. Suddenly, out of the corner of my eye, I spot this young, shy woman, who couldn't be more than 18 or 19, looking up at me. I can see fear in her eyes, but I can also see hope. My topic is about breaking free of subconscious fears, and I'm being my own laboratory! In a split-second, I realize this is about being here to serve this young woman and every single person in this audience who came to break free. I can't do that if I'm letting the fear stop me. This is part of my purpose, to break free myself and then help others. Life wants me here, and I have to trust the wisdom of that. There is an order and a sequence to everything. At that moment, the fear vanishes and it is like this wiser part of me is now speaking. I feel confident and charismatic and more myself than ever before. It's like my energy is filling up the entire room. I can actually see the stress melting from people's faces and being replaced by confidence, belief, and inspiration.

I end my presentation by saying "The greatest tragedy is not dying but dying with your music still in you." Suddenly I'm getting a standing ovation. They are rushing up and saying, "That changed my life, I'm so glad I was here so that I could receive that message."

That's how quick you can go from insecurity to confidence, by remembering that you are there to serve people. Self-consciousness is actually a form of self-centeredness. It's putting your attention on yourself too much. Once you are "Other-Conscious," often the awkwardness, fear, and disconnection melts away.

Here are three tips that will help you to remember to care for your listeners.

Tip #1 – Who are they?

Even though we covered this when you did the groundwork, it is important each time you present to think about who will be listening and then make slight adjustments to the presentation to make it fit for them and their needs. You can tap into them intuitively, and you can also find things out before and during the presentation.

Here are five quick things to consider.

1. **The age or age range of your listeners.** This helps you gear your examples and stories the right way. For example, you don't want to talk about a seventies TV show to people born after 1995.

2. **Main roles or responsibilities.** For example, parent, real estate agent, retiree.

3. **Goals that Your Company Can Help Them Achieve.** For example, leaving their job, being home more with their children, having a second income.

4. **Challenges that Your Company Can Help Them Overcome.** For example, no savings for retirement, long commute to work.

5. **Top Interests in Life**. For example, health & fitness, time with family, ability to travel and have a more flexible lifestyle

Tip #2 - Are they comfortable?

This is something that can easily be forgotten. If people can't see you or hear you properly, then the presentation is doomed from the start. Maybe the seating is uncomfortable, it's too hot, or too cold, or they are hungry or thirsty or need to use the restroom. It's harder for people to pay attention when basic needs have not been met. Before presenting make sure that you have asked yourself these four questions

> 1. How can you ensure there is little or no competing noise?
>
> 2. How can you ensure you have their full attention?
>
> 3. How can you ensure they are comfortable?
>
> 4. How can you ensure they can see you and your visuals?

Tip #3 - Are YOU Listening?

Are you more focused on your notes than on them? Are you rattling on at high speed for too long without asking them a question or letting it sink in?

Here are four questions you can ask yourself, to ensure that you are listening.

> **1. How can I make sure I PAUSE from time to time?** Pausing helps people catch up, and it gathers attention. It forces you to slow down and see if they are still with you.
>
> **2. What kinds of questions can I ask to make sure they are understanding? For example:**
> - What are your thoughts so far?
> - How do you see this working in your life?

3. What kinds of questions can I ask to find out their objections and concerns?
- What are your concerns about joining at this time?
- What's in the way for you?

4. How can I make sure I pay attention to non-verbal signals? If they're crossing their arms, looking away or looking at their watch, then you probably need to check in with them.

Mistake #2- Resisting People's Resistance

What do I mean by that? No matter how experienced you are as a presenter, people will feel resistance to your products, services, ideas, and opportunities. It's just a natural human inclination to be skeptical about new ideas and opportunities. It's actually a safety valve for most people. Otherwise, you can feel bombarded every day.

If you're afraid of their resistance, you may ignore it, push it away, or get defensive. That's going to block your success. You are better off to expect it and be totally ok with it. Without proper preparation, your survival brain can get triggered and then you can end up speaking too fast, being too pushy, or forgetting what you want to say.

Why do people resist? Check out these four reasons and see if you can remember a time any of these were true for you.

1. INERTIA: There is a natural inertia in people when it comes to doing something new or being open to new possibilities.

2. FEAR OF BEING MANIPULATED: There are presenters who manipulate people, and so people are naturally on guard for that.

3. SUSPICION OF STRANGERS: Many of us were taught to distrust strangers. If you are a stranger to them, or others in the room are strangers, you will need to break the ice and prove good intent.

4. POWERLESSNESS: You are the one with the control as the presenter. Many people naturally resist when others have the control in a social situation.

Here are four ways to transform resistance:

1. Normalize their resistance. For example, admit to feeling resistant yourself when you first joined the business. Reassure them that it's normal and that you're ok with it. This will help them let down their guard.

2. Prove your good intent. Go into the meeting feeling unattached to the outcome, because people can sense desperation a mile away. Make it clear that you have no interest in manipulating them into something that's not a good fit. Reassure them that you just want to help them, if it makes sense in their life now. If not, no hard feelings. Either way is fine.

3. Icebreakers. Facilitate them getting to know you and other participants. Your personal story can help with this. Non-threatening icebreaker games can help them get to know others.

4. Check in with them. Give the power back to the listener by suggesting an agenda and time frame and asking their permission to proceed. You can also ask for their comments and questions throughout, which allows them to help mold the presentation to their needs.

Mistake # 3 - Lack of Proper Rehearsal

I was watching an interview show called *Inside the Actor's Studio*. They often discuss the technical aspects of acting, a lot of which also applies to presenting

William H. Macy is a really amazing acting teacher as well as an actor. He was saying that acting is very stressful. When you get stressed, you go into the survival brain and then you lose access to your whole brain.

If you've rehearsed your lines over and over again, even if you're stressed out, you'll still be able to access the important information. A way to transform this situation is to develop habits as an actor or presenter, not only of what you're going to say but of how you're going to BE as you deliver the words.

Let's look at ways to develop important delivery habits.

Script your presentation

There are five reasons to do this.

>**1. You'll see the structure of your presentation.** People are more engaged if your presentation has an underlying structure. If you just wander from one topic to the next and back again, people may find that frustrating. If you haven't written it out, then you can't see if there is a good structure. A script allows you to see where you are repeating yourself, where you are going too long without using stories or examples, or where you've skipped important information.
>
>**2. It makes you feel more confident.** If you take the time to script it out and edit it, then you will feel like you are giving good value to your listener. If a person just "wings it" or makes a few notes ahead of time, sometimes they can do ok if they are a seasoned presenter and if they really know their topic. Most people, however, come across as less professional when they "wing it". As such, you may notice your listener be less engaged, and this can negatively affect your confidence, and business growth.

3. It helps you remember what you want to say in the moment. If you are presenting live, try not to read your script unless you can do so and still remain very connected to your audience. Many people who read a script start to sound monotonous. If you think that might happen then just bold certain parts of the script to help trigger the thought of the next paragraph. If you CAN read a script and bring aliveness to your voice, this will help your confidence.

4. It will help you remember for next time. For example, say you presented your business opportunity on March 3rd for five people in your home. Then you decide to do that again on May 15th. Chances are you will have forgotten what you said because it's been three months. Even if you had an outline, you probably won't know what your bullet points mean anymore.

5. It will help you improve. If the presentation didn't go well, you can look at the script and deconstruct what you said and make it better. You can't improve what you can't measure.

Record Yourself

Top presenters audio and video tape themselves before and during a presentation. Rehearse into an audio recorder and listen back. Rehearse in front of your video camera or webcam and watch it. You'll learn a lot about what you like and what you want to improve. Then, during a 1-to-1, see if you can audiotape it. For larger presentations, see if you can videotape it. You can do this with your iPhone. Just ask permission from people if you're talking one-to-one. You can say, "Do you mind if I record this? It's just for my own sake." Then listen back. You will hear and see what works. Maybe you are powerful in the beginning and when telling your personal story. You will also hear and see what doesn't work. Maybe during the company story, you said 'um' every three words and sound stilted. That way you know what to work on.

Why do this? Because you are often not aware in the moment. You're just focused on getting the information out. You're not aware that you're saying "um" far too often. The recordings will help you improve better than anything else.

Mental Rehearsal

Pro athletes discovered mental rehearsal in the 1940s. If a hockey player imagined himself getting a goal in his mind, his goals more than doubled. You can do the same thing with giving presentations by programming your subconscious mind for success using all your senses. For example, you can imagine that your voice is clear and engaging. You can imagine yourself feeling calm and centered and remembering everything you wanted to say. You can see yourself acting in a confident and professional way. You can feel yourself breathing, pausing and asking questions. You can hear yourself normalizing their resistance. Do it for one minute a few times leading up to your actual presentation, and you'll notice a big improvement.

If you try the mental rehearsal and it works, come over to my Facebook page **https://www.facebook.com/carlarieger** and let me know. I love to hear success stories!

Mistake #4 - Trying to Do It Alone

You are smart to be reading this book today. It's challenging to improve by yourself, so that's why reading books, taking courses, getting coaching, recording yourself, doing practice sessions with friends, helps you so much.

One thing that's great about network marketing is it's designed for people to help each other. Now I know your upline may or may not be available all the time. However, you can also ask other people in your company or someone outside your company. In fact, sometimes those kinds of people are more helpful because they'll be listening to your presentation with fresh eyes.

As Margaret Wheatley says, "*Nothing living lives alone.*" We all need help to grow our business. We need help to grow our skills, and that's one reason Dave O'Connor and I created The Network Marketing Leadership Academy, or NMLA for short. Just go to **www.NMLA.biz** and check it out.

Presentation Skills for Prosperity

We created this because we felt like, for many people, they need extra skill building to augment what they're already getting in their company. We see network marketing as a profession, like being a financial planner, or realtor. You actually cannot perform those roles without getting proper, certified training. Yet, in the network marketing and direct selling world, there are no credentials to get. This is a good thing and a bad thing. It lowers the barrier to entry, but it also means lots of people are out there trying to succeed without the proper training.

Your confidence improves massively when you take the time to learn the skills to succeed in your business. Even if you just create practice groups in your team. You can get together with four people, and you can just rehearse your presentation with each other.
If you avoid these four mistakes, you will instantly have more confidence when you talk with people. And they will be more apt to listen and join your business.

Now in chapter 8 we are going to look at something that affects every person no matter how prepared you are and that is the pre-performance nerves. We'll look at what you can do to minimize those nerves and make them work FOR you instead of against you.

Chapter 8 - How to Transform Anxiety as a Presenter

Bill stood behind the stage feeling like he was going to throw up. His stomach was in knots, and his hands were shaking so badly that he kept dropping his notes. "How am I ever going to do this?"

When Bill was young, he was smaller than most of the boys his age and wore glasses. In school, he was invited to do a book report at the front of the room. He could barely get a word out, and the other students laughed at him. The teacher did nothing to prepare him ahead of time on how to do it properly, nor how to improve it for next time. This is a very common scenario that creates public speaking phobias in adults.

A few decades later, Bill is now a tall, strong and handsome network marketer. People love being around him, and his network marketing business is growing quickly, because of his wonderful ability to communicate with people one-to-one. Then he gets asked by head office to give a presentation at the company convention on how he built his business so quickly. That's when the memories of his childhood kick back in. Back then he decided he was bad at public speaking even though he only tried it once and never had any training. Most people are bad at things on their first try, especially with no training.

That's when he sought out help. I was able to help him de-program that belief and get the training to be a good presenter in front of groups. He learned what I am going to teach you in this chapter.

Most people get the jitters, even people who have been doing it for 30 years can get nervous. It's completely normal. It's what you do with it that determines success or failure in your presentation. There is a spectrum of the human condition when it comes to public speaking. On one side, you have intense anxiety where your hands are shaking, you get flop sweat, and you can't remember what you're going to say, and so on. Then on the other side of the spectrum, it total boredom. I'm sure you've seen presenters that seem like they don't care. They're just doing it out of obligation.

Then there is a sweet spot in the middle which is what I call "nervous excitement." You are a bit nervous because you care. You care that it goes well and that you are your best self and can really give good value to people. And you're excited because you believe in your material, you want to help people and you believe in yourself and your ability to add value to their lives. Therefore, everything in this chapter is about getting you more and more towards the sweet spot.

In this chapter, we will look at how to avoid the top two mistakes many network marketing presenters make when it come to overcoming anxiety.

Mistake #1 – Comparing Yourself Negatively to Others

Many people look at good presenters and feel intimidated. At one point, those good presenters were bad and just learned how to get better. Instead, study them. They might be part of your company, or not. What are they doing that you really like? How can you incorporate what they say, and how they say it, into your presentation?

This doesn't mean copying them word-for-word, but rather letting them inspire you. Analyze what they are doing that is helping them succeed. This research may also help build your competitive spirit to see how to make your presentations even better, or different by adding something unique.

You can also see which target markets they are approaching and which ones they are not targeting. It might challenge you to specifically niche yourself to a certain type of person. The more specific you niche yourself, the easier it can be to launch your business, or build to the next level quickly.

So make a list of three presenters you can study. This is a great way to see why the are so successful. Go to their website and read their blogs. Sign up and listen to their webinars or watch their videos. Follow them on social media and watch what they do that gets results. Go to a live presentation and watch their body language. Analyze what they do to relate to the audience.

Interview them on the phone or in person. People love to share their wisdom if you give them a specific time limit and let them do most of the talking. Here's an example of what you can ask them.

> 1. Who are your ideal prospects and what do you initially say to get them interested in learning more?
>
> 2. What helps you give good presentations?
>
> 3. What do you say that seems to make the most difference to people finally joining?

Mistake #2 – Allowing Negative Self Talk to Take Over

Here is a technique that is great for overcoming negative self-talk when it comes to giving presentations. It's easy to do in everyday life. It gets you immediately into a new state of mind. Before looking at this technique, it helps first to understand where public speaking anxiety comes from.

We need to look at the behaviour and trace it back to the emotion, the thought and then to the core belief. For example, I had a client, named Beth, that once went completely blank during a presentation to 100 people. She completely forgot what she wanted to say and got flustered, turned red, and started having a coughing fit. Eventually, she had to apologize and end the presentation early. Every since then, she has avoided public speaking.

I first asked what emotion was fuelling that behavior and not surprisingly, it was anxiety. Knowing that, however, doesn't solve the problem. We had to explore where that emotion came from. It doesn't just appear out of nowhere. It comes from a thought, right? Her underlying thought was, *what if this goes badly, very badly*? She was letting gremlin voices whisper subconsciously to her and believing them.

When that happened it triggering her survival brain. When the survival brain gets triggered, it cuts off your thinking ability, voice, and coordination. And even though she tried to "will" herself not to worry, it wasn't working.

Why do some people worry like that when giving presentations, and some people don't? That thought - *what if this goes badly, very badly* – was being fueled by a CORE

BELIEF. After a bit of digging we discovered that, in her case, the core belief was *public speaking is dangerous*.

After ten years of coaching people at all levels of experience, I hear the same kind of situation over and over gain. That core belief often gets formed in our childhood. Like Bill's story of having to do the book report.

In Beth's case, she was 10 years old and suddenly invited to read a Shakespeare monologue at the front of the room. She stumbled over the words, and the teacher criticized her in front of everyone. Beth then made a decision that giving presentations leads to public humiliation and is, therefore, dangerous. She didn't remember making that decision, but it got lodged in her subconscious. Her subconscious is now just trying to protect her from public humiliation again, so it triggers the survival response when in a similar situation as an adult.

Now, somebody who doesn't go blank might have a different core belief such as *public speaking is safe*. If you do get anxious, you may have an unconscious program that says public speaking is dangerous. The important thing to know is that there are ways to turn it around and create new and more supportive core beliefs.

There are different theories about why people consider public speaking dangerous. From your survival brain's perspective, it sees that you might die. In our early tribal days, if you lost the approval of the tribe, you got expelled and had to try to survive on your own and most people couldn't survive that. Tribal approval, therefore, is still hard wired into the survival brain even though in today's culture you would still physically survive if you did poorly at public speaking.

If you've ever tried to intellectually talk to yourself out of worrying, of seeing life through this core belief, you know how hard it can be. You have to go to the source code, the back end programming, redirect the loop in a positive direction.

You can try this next exercise and see if it works for you. It has worked for hundreds of people I've worked with including myself. I use it regularly, and it only takes a few minutes. Just think of a presentation situation coming up that's making you anxious or at least a bit uncomfortable.

Before we start, just rate yourself between 1 and 10 in terms of anxiety on this issue. 1 is no anxiety, and 10 is massive anxiety. Now list all worries and concerns regarding an upcoming presentation using 'what if' to start your sentence. See examples below.

Negative "What if's":
- What if I mess up?
- What if people seem resistant?
- What if I can't remember what I want to say?
- What if my voice sounds weird?
- What if people think I'm boring?
- What if I freeze up?
- What if I run out of time?

Now write out 'what if' plus the opposite or positive outcome.

Positive "What if's":
- What if I do well?
- What if people seem open minded?
- What if I CAN remember what I want to say?
- What if my voice sounds good?
- What if people think I'm interesting?
- What if I seem confident?
- What if I end on time?

Writing those out and reading them over and over again, people notice their whole system just calms down. It overrides the survival brain. There is a third option if this doesn't work, and that is a neutral "What if."

Neutral "What if's":
- What if I mess up, and it's ok, I learn and move on?
- What if people seem resistant, and it's ok, I learn and move on?
- What if I can't remember what I want to say, and it's ok, I learn and move on?
- What if my voice sounds weird, and it's ok, I learn and move on?
- What if people think I'm boring, and it's ok, I learn and move on?
- What if I freeze up, and it's ok, I learn and move on?
- What if I run out of time, and it's ok, I learn and move on?

Inevitably some things will go wrong. And if you have the attitude that you are willing to learn from the situation and just get better for next time – this can also calm down the survival brain. Just look back on your life and all the mistakes you've made. Chances are generally it was ok, you learned and moved on, right?

Another thing you can do is go back to the inciting incident (usually in childhood). Be there with the child and empathize with her and coach her.

For example:

I understand why you would feel that public speaking is dangerous. That was an unpleasant experience and so it's normal for you to feel bad about it.

Another perspective to consider is, public speaking can be safe. You may just need more practice. That teacher just isn't very skilled at helping people like you succeed. But you can get the help now and vindicate yourself. Want to try?

Sometimes this helps your subconscious mind which is often controlled by the "inner child", break free and make a new decision.

My Story of Transformation

Let me give you an example of how I was able to transform quite a lot of anxiety as a presenter for a high-stakes presentation situation.

I was hired to lead a workshop at a cancer center back in the 1990's, and it was near the beginning of my professional speaking career, so it was what I would call a *character building experience*. My topic was "The Healing Effect of Laughter in a Healthcare Setting." Now, this was when the concept that positive emotions could help you get healthy, was new to western medicine. I'd done a lot of research, and I wanted to spread the message.

I really believed in it, but I was also quite young and naive about the ways of the world at that time. The woman who hired me was new on the job as a human resources manager. She didn't know about getting permission from the right people before hiring someone like me, and she also didn't tell me about the politics going on behind the scenes.

When I get up to the front of the room to begin my presentation, I notice a row of doctors sitting at the back of the room with their arms crossed, peering at me over reading glasses with aloof looks of disdain. About ten minutes into my presentation, one interrupts me mid-sentence and says, "What makes you think that we have time in our highly intense schedule to be joking around with a patient? There's absolutely no empirical evidence to suggest that laughing improves a person's immune system. Do YOU have a Ph.D. in this subject?"

It catches me off guard and so I kind of freeze like a deer in the headlights. There is an awkward silence. Even though I was well researched on the topic, I am thinking, I don't think you can get a doctorate in laughter. I then think – I probably should NOT tell them that I only have a Bachelor's degree in English literature.

Finally, I say, "Here's a statistic about a children's hospital in Ohio that has a humour room. The humour room is full of books, and videos and cartoons. A clown comes once a day and does magic tricks. The researchers tested a variety of vital functions in the kids and found their immune system improved by 65% with only ten minutes of laughing."

"That's ALL your evidence?" the doctor retorts.

"I have other evidence," I say as I search through my notes. Then, one-by-one the doctors leave the room. After about five minutes, two-thirds of the room had left and one-third stayed. Those who remained were nurses who liked the topic and believed in it. But, by that time I was so shaken. When your confidence is shaken, of course, your presentation skills diminish greatly. I got consumed by anxiety and self-doubt from having been the recipient of that public disapproval, which is that thing the survival brain hates the most.

I was shocked by how much it affected me not only on the day, but it went on for months. I was seriously considering changing careers, just so I never had to experience that again. Then something happened that changed my whole relationship with being a presenter. It was a game changer.

I worked with a coach at that time to deal with it, and I told her my story of public disapproval, and she told me a story. She says to me, "Did you know that Copernicus said the world was round and he was condemned to death for it? Galileo confirmed his findings and people put him in prison for the rest of his life. Then, many years later, Newton confirmed it again at a time in history when everyone was finally ready to accept it, and so he was given an award."

"Have you chosen this career to get people's approval or to make a difference in people's lives?" Now, I could feel the negative voices inside having a war about the answer to that question. She said, "You must choose which road you are on and feed that road with all your attention."

Therefore, I made a decision that day to choose the high road, to make a difference in people's lives despite the pushback. It wasn't easy for me, and I receive plenty more public disapproval and pushback over the next few years. But ironically, ten years after I did that presentation, that same cancer clinic was in the news because they were having laughter yoga practitioners come in on a regular basis.

Presentation Skills for Prosperity

One of the nurses who had seen me speak continued to bring forth the idea, year after year, until finally it was accepted. The truth is, whenever you stand in front of a group of people, or you talk to somebody about a business opportunity, you're going to get resistance, you're going to get disapproval.

In fact, if you're not "ruffling some feathers" and challenging people in some way, you may not be doing your job properly. I can't tell you how many times I heard people say, "I went into this network marketing thing kicking and screaming, and it's ended up being the best thing that ever happened in my life." If you can deal with resistance in people in this kind of setting, you can do it with anything in your life. And sometimes people will later thank you profusely for continuing to make the offer in the face of their consistent rejection.

The intensity of that experience with the cancer centre changed my need for approval at a core level. It changed the source code. I either had to keep the need for approval, or give it up and have the career I said I wanted. And that point, I had already put so much of my time and energy into it, that it didn't make sense to give it up. Staying safe would lead me to feeling off purpose. Being ON purpose became a higher priority for me and has kept me moving forward ever since.

In Chapter 9 we are going to dive into how to captivate your audience and really take your presentation to the next level. You will learn how to be able to speak to a big group of people and have all of them feel like you are talking to them individually at the same time.

Chapter 9: Captivating Your Audience

Have you ever spoken to a group of people and watched their reactions? What did you see? More than likely you saw a range of reactions. Some people seem engaged, some people are taking notes, some people look confused, some seem bored.

Why is one group getting it and the other isn't? Because whether it was intentional or not, a presentation is often created to reach a certain group of people who are most like the presenter. It's just a natural human tendency.

We all fall into different categories, whether that be male or female, introvert or extrovert or things like brain dominance and learning styles. All these things make us unique and will affect how we receive communication. You need to take that into account when creating your presentations so that they reach the most people.

Why do people seem unengaged at times? Guess what is the average adult attention span is these days? One hour, 15 minutes? According to statistics, the average adult attention span is actually only seven seconds. Every seven seconds you take a mental break. You think about something else. In fact, you could be actually taking a mental break right now! LOL

As Chip Heath, author of the best-selling book, *Made To Stick*, said, "The first problem of communication is getting people's attention." But also as Philip Randolph once said, "It's easy to get people's attention, what counts is getting their interest."

The personal touch in network marketing, referral-based businesses, is that you need to take all that information and create meaning for people. Machines, websites, robotic phone messages can't do it like you can.

Left Brain/Right Brain Dominance

In Chapter 6, I introduced to you the concept of left brain/right brain dominance, and in this chapter, I want to go into it further. Now if you are like most people, you are probably wondering which is your dominant brain. Check out this quick little quiz to find out.

Presentation Skills for Prosperity

1. You have five projects to complete in two weeks. How do you go about completing them?

    a. I list the projects in order of importance and work on each, one by one, until completion.
    b. I just jump into whichever project is appealing and work on all of them piece by piece until they get done.
    c. I organize them in order of importance but switch between projects as I go.

2. You've signed up to learn a language such as French. What's the best way for you to learn?

    a. I need to start by memorizing the vocabulary and verbal conjugations.
    b. I need to repeat after a teacher and be immersed in conversation with native speakers.
    c. I need to switch back and forth between memorizing and practicing.

3. You bring home a Kitchen Blender that looks complicated to use. What do you do?

    a. I read the instruction manual, step-by-step, before trying it out.
    b. I try out the buttons until I figure out how it works.
    c. I quickly glance through the instruction manual and then try it out.

4. It's time to do your taxes. Where are all your financial documents and receipts?

>a. Filed away neatly, organized by date.
>b. All over the place, and you're really not sure where to find it all.
>c. In a mess, but all in the same place.

5. You are shopping for a new car. How do you make your decision?

>a. Research the car you want and make price comparisons.
>b. Sit in the car, test drive it, to see if it feels right.
>c. Do a bit of research, and take it for a test drive to see how it feels.

6. When it came to following rules as a child, your parents or teachers would probably say that:

>a. You were mostly well behaved and generally didn't question them.
>b. You would question many rules in place: "but why do I have to?"
>c. You were generally respectful of the rules, but sometimes questioned them.

So count how many A's, B's and C's you have. Which one was more? If you have more:

Presentation Skills for Prosperity

A's - You are left brain dominant
B's - You are right brain dominant
C's - You are balanced between both

People who are left brained tend to THINK more and people who are right brained tend to FEEL more. In most presentations, the group will be split 50/50 you want to make sure that you reach both groups in your presentation. You don't want to lose 50% of your potential customers and team members just because YOU prefer one over the other. That is why preparation is important.

Now we already covered in chapter 6 the different types of things you want to include in your presentations so that you reach both groups. But I wanted to give you a quick tip, especially when it comes to left brained people. ALWAYS CHECK YOUR FACTS AND STATISTICS, and don't just check them on Wikipedia.

Remember I told you back at the beginning of the chapter that the average adult attention span is only 7 seconds? I heard someone say that and I so I checked it on Wikipedia. However, journalists never use Wikipedia as it is not always written by professional researchers. It's mostly written by volunteers. Once someone from my audience shouted out, *I think you're wrong about that statistic*!

That's when I learned about Google Scholar.
When I typed in 'average adult attention span' to Google Scholar I found three references to it being between 18 and 20 minutes. These tend to be scientific-based studies. And if

you are ever talking to someone who is very left brained and scientific they will appreciate that you've done your proper research, and will not appreciate if you are just spouting statistics that you heard someone else say.

V.A.R.K.

The other thing you want to consider when creating and delivering your presentations is people's learning styles. There are four main ones. Some people are **Visual**, others are **Auditory**, others are what's called **Read\Write**, and others are **Kinesthetic**.

That said, most people are what's called *multimodality learners*, meaning they like to learn in a variety of modes and a variety of formats for the information to stick. You want to make sure that you include elements from each of these learning styles into your presentation, to reach as many people as possible.

Let's take a look at each one and how you can incorporate it into your presentation.

Visual Learners

Visual learners like presenters who use gestures and picturesque language. An example of picturesque language would be the metaphor of a prism and showing a visual image of it on a slide. Visual learners like videos, slides, flip charts, graphs, flowcharts. Even if you are talking one-to-one, you might want to have brochures or a slide show to share. How do you tell if someone is a visual learner? They use words like *I see what you mean*, or *I can picture that*.

Auditory Learners

Auditory learners like to ask questions and have conversations. Make sure you don't do all the talking, but you keep checking in with and asking them to apply what you're talking about into their life. Auditory learners also like to listen to an audio presentation about your company as opposed to a video. Or talk on the phone or participate in a teleseminar. You might hear them say – *I hear what you're saying,* or *let me summarize what I heard.*

Read/Write Learners

Read\write learners like to see material with written descriptions, make notes, do background research, use worksheets or fill in quizzes. You might hear them say – *let me just make some notes* or *Do you have all this written out somewhere?*

Kinesthetic Learners

Kinesthetic learners like stories that involve all the senses. They like to taste test your products. The want to learn through experience. They like case studies of real people. They like a field trip to the head office. You might hear them say things like – *I feel excited about this opportunity*, or *can I try the product?* It's feeling language; it's language where they clearly want to get involved in some way before they make a decision.

Getting Better Results

When you take the time to incorporate all these things into your presentations, you are going to notice a big difference in your results. More people will pay attention to what you say and take action on it. When you do presentations to larger groups, you will have people come up to you at the end and tell you how much it meant to them. It is an art form, and the great thing is that anyone can learn it. Over time you can become a master of it.

Now it is time to put it all together.

Chapter 10: Putting It All Together

How are you feeling right now? Excited and can't wait to get started and also maybe overwhelmed and not sure where to start?

As we tie everything together in this last chapter, I want to start with something that is very important to remember, and that is…

It's A Process

Becoming an amazing presenter for your products and opportunity takes time, it doesn't just fall into your lap. The great thing is that you have an advantage over everyone else trying to wing it alone. You read this book and have the basics you need to get started on presenting it right THE FIRST TIME around.

BUT!

What if you still feel uncomfortable with doing this yourself. Maybe English wasn't your best class, or you have all these ideas, and you are just not sure how to put them together into a coherent form. If that is you, then help is just one click away. Go to www.NMLA.biz and check out **The Network Marketing Leadership Academy**. Not only will you get more training on how to implement everything in this book, but you will also get to ask questions to personalize this information just for you, and you get to win points and rewards, and you get to attend one of our live events.

The Checklist

Are you a checklist person? Do you love having everything laid out for you step-by-step so that you know where to start? If that is you, you will love this next section.

☑ **1. Choose what type of presentation you want to do**. One-to-one, small group or large group.

☑ **2. Do the Presentation Goals Clarity Process**. Do this process in Chapter 3 and figure out your personal vision, the right niche and then how to serve that niche.

☑ **3. Create a Story**. Unless you are just creating your one-minute mission statement, you want to create your Why

Story first as you will be using this in most types of presentations that you do.

☑ **4. Outline Your Presentation**. After you have your story, create the rest of the presentation around it. You can use point forms or write it out in full if you want to use it over and over again.

☑ **5. Connect to Your Listeners**. Go back and check to see if it is still in line with number one, knowing your listeners and who it is you are going to be speaking too.

☑ **6. Practice, Practice and practice** some more. Record it, practice it in front of other people and get their feedback and then change what needs to be changed.

☑ **7. Refine your Presentation**. Now that you have your basics go back through and make sure that you have elements in it that not only appeal to both left brain/right brain dominance but learning styles as well.

☑ **8. Practice, Practice and Practice** some more. Yes, I already said that, but I cannot stress how important it is. Memorize the opening, your closing and your story at the minimum so that you can say it naturally and you don't have to think about.

☑ **9. Build Your Confidence**. If you know that you have anxiety as a presenter, then go back through Chapter 8 and do the exercise there. If this is something that you need to work on, don't put it off. You can have the greatest presentation ever, but if you can't physically get it out when the time comes, what good is that going to do you?

☑ **10. Have Fun**. Remember have fun with this, treat it like a game, and as you grow your skills, you'll learn to love giving presentations if you don't already feel that way now. Giving great presentations will help you reap huge results especially the more you love it.

I would love to hear how it goes for you. Come on over to Facebook **https://www.facebook.com/carlarieger** and share with me your success.

I hope that this has been an incredible journey for you as it has been for me. I love to help people succeed in Network Marketing, and this book has been a part of that.

I highly encourage you to take the D.A.N.C.E. Personality Style Quiz **http://carlarieger.com/MLMDANCEQUIZ** That way you can increase your conversions by up to 75% while also finding a way of prospecting and marketing your business that works for you, thereby having more joy, less stress and more income.

You can do this. No matter what you are feeling right now, take that first step, it's easy. The only bad decision you can make is not to start at all. Everything else is just the part of the learning process.

Have the courage to make your dreams come true. Who knows maybe one day you will be standing on a stage sharing your story of transforming obstacles and achieving your goals. That would be a dream come true for me. Until then what are you waiting for?

GET STARTED.

Who Is Carla Rieger?

Carla helps leaders become innovative communicators and presenters.

She began her career with an innovative teambuilding company in the US in 1988 called Playfair, Inc. Since then she has spoken to over 1500 groups internationally of up to 4000 people. In 1991 she became the director of The Artistry of Change Training & Coaching Inc., a firm that specializes in awakening creative potentials in people so that they can be strong presenters and communicators.

In terms of formal education, Carla has an undergraduate in English, Psychology and Theatre and graduate work in Organizational Development. She also has extensive training in adult education, leadership and conflict resolution. She has been a fitness instructor, natural healing consultant, Educational Kinesiology instructor, mediator, and presentation skills coach.

On the artistic side she has performed in dozens of plays and musicals, written seven plays, a screenplay and a novel. Her specialty has been theatrical improvisation and Carla has founded three theatre troupes. In non-fiction she has written four books on change, conflict resolution and presentation skills, over 80 online learning programs, as well as over 100 articles that have appeared in a wide variety of journals.

She has 22 years of research and experience in such diverse areas as:

- Applied kinesiology
- Adult education
- Neuro Linguistic Programming
- Self hypnosis
- Change management
- Drama therapy
- Playback Theatre
- Psychodrama
- Creative process theory
- Personality styles
- Conflict resolution
- Sociometry
- Organizational development
- Western and Eastern practices to develop human potential

Why was The Artistry of Change Inc. created?

After years of surveying and interviewing change leaders and visionary business owners we noticed that those with training in the arts seemed to be better at manifesting their visions in the real world. Because at its core, the creative process and the change process are one and the same.

Thus, the Artistry of Change was born. That is why Carla Rieger focuses on bringing secrets from the world of the arts into leadership, particularly when presenting to groups and having conversations that open minds to new ideas.

Her work as a speaker, trainer, author, and performer has been featured on radio, TV and in magazines. As a frequent presenter before all types of groups internationally, Carla helps them communicate their message with integrity, authenticity and creativity.

What makes our offerings different than others?

-We deal with issues at core levels for long-term results versus only short term
-We use leading-edge processes versus out-of-date ones
-We can customize to your needs rather than only offer a one-size fits all version
-We have an engaging delivery style versus a dry and boring one
-We offer practical solutions versus just vague concepts

What does Artistry of Change mean?

Sounds flakey, doesn't it? What is an artist of change? People, organizations and governments are investing heavily in building greater creative capacities in people. As such there is a growing movement all over the world of people stepping forward to enhance creative capacity to solve the complex problems of the world we now face. Old solutions are quickly becoming obsolete as our world changes at an exponential rate.

Therefore, we are now in an age ruled by artistry, empathy and emotion. Many school systems tend to invalidate creative abilities, so the work world today is filled with people who don't remember how to be creative.

The Artistry of Change® model awakens natural creativity, emotional intelligence and communication skills quickly. These processes show you the steps necessary to bring your best self to serve others. This is an innovative approach that blends the best of diverse fields such as business, arts, science and communication. Witness how those fields are merging in exciting new ways and allowing people to become the artists of their lives…manifesting the fulfillment, income, and impact they seek.

Connect with Carla
www.CarlaRieger.com
https://www.facebook.com/carlarieger
https://twitter.com/carlarieger
https://www.instagram.com/riegercarla
https://es.pinterest.com/carlarieger/
https://www.linkedin.com/in/carlarieger

The Artistry of Change Training & Consulting Inc.
Visit us on the web: www.ArtistryofChange.com
E-Mail: Carla@ArtistryofChange.com

www.ingramcontent.com/pod-product-compliance
Lightning Source LLC
Chambersburg PA
CBHW070254190526
45169CB00001B/407